Sacred Symbols of Light

by Jean Logan, Ph.D.

There is a new language of Light that is coming on to the planet.

Copyright 2012 by Jean Logan
Second Edition 2017

All rights reserved. No part of this book may be reproduced or utilized in any form or by any means, electronic or mechanical, including photocopying and recording or by any information storage and retrieval system, without permission in writing from the publisher except at noted on page 4.

Published by Holy Ground Farm, Inc.

Cover and book design by Bull's-Eye Creative Communications
Chakra Drawings by Dan Winner

ISBN 978-1-61364-581-9

Printed in China through Four Colour Imports USA

Dedication

This work is dedicated with gratitude to the I Am Presence.

This book and the glyphs contained herein are empowered with the violet flame of St. Germain. St. Germain has attached an aspect of himself to each manual including those electronically reproduced.

Message from St. Germain.

"Listen to your heart. Know that I am with you always. My love is genuine. Hold the flame of that love to your heart. See the Divine in all your brothers and sisters. Know that your path is chosen. Mark the time for it will come to pass. I want you to understand that your duty is to the beloved I Am Presence in all things. I see you naked before the dawn. I see your sorrows and know the love in your heart. Contemplate the meaning of all you do to see that it corresponds with the purpose for your being here."

All of the proceeds from this manual are used to help our work with disadvantaged children. If your friends would like a copy, please encourage them to buy their own copy or make a donation to cover any copies given out to others. Your spiritual integrity in this matter is very much appreciated.

The holder of a valid receipt for the purchase of this manual has permission to have copies made of any of the images inside the manual.

Many blessings and enjoy the use of these glyphs.

Contents

Introduction

Sacred Symbols of Light

Using the Glyphs

11. Circulatory System Clearing and Healing. 17
12. Urethra and Bladder Clearing 21
20. Bones and Cartilage Regeneration 25
21. Pituitary, Thalamus, Hypothalamus and Pineal. . 29
28. Remove Vaccinations 33
31. Vertebrae Support 37
32. Stomach, Liver, Gallbladder and Pancreas 41
33. Adrenal Glands and Kidney Support 45
34. Clear Vision 49
35. Hearing/Ear/Olfactory 53
36. Spleen Healing and Support 57
37. Heart Healing and Support. 61
38. Lungs Healing and Support 65
39. Female Reproductive System. 69
40. Restore Surgically Removed Adenoids 73
41. Muscle Restoration 77
43. Skin Restoration 81
44. Detoxification II 85
45. Male Reproductive System 89

47. Thymus Regeneration and Support 93
48. Restore Thyroid Gland 97
57. Resolve Nerve Damage 101
60. Remove Etheric Implants 105
69. Malignant Growths 109
70. Expansion of Consciousness 113
72. Marijuana 117
86. Electromagnetic Frequencies 121
88. Abscessed Tooth 125
89. Restore Surgically Removed Tonsils 129
93. Candida and Intestinal Support 133
94. Allergies 137
95. Lymphatic Cleansing 141
96. Resolving Neurological Problems 145
97. Checkerboard - Spiritual Enhancement 149
99. Energize Dantian and Snow Mountain 153

Appendix A - Locating the Chakras 157
Appendix B - AcuTapping 159
Appendix C - Dowsing 161
Appendix D - Testimonials 167
Appendix E - Resolving Brain Damage 173
Appendix F - Assistance Program for Children 175
Appendix G - Suggested Reading 177
Appendix H - Reading by Judith Moore 179
Appendix I - Disclaimer 181

Introduction

For the benefit of those who have not read my first book "*Unlocking the Power of Glyphs,*" I am repeating much of the same information in the Introduction in order to help everyone understand what glyphs are all about. First of all, I want to explain what a glyph is. According to Webster's Dictionary, a glyph is "a symbol that conveys information non verbally." One internet definition site defined it as "a symbol or character, especially one that has been incised or carved out in a stone surface like the characters of the ancient Maya writing system."

A few years ago I received an e-mail from a friend that contained a glyph. The glyph was a small drawing of some type of insect with a wavy line around it. The author of the glyph wrote under it, "Restoring Divine DNA Blueprint." She also wrote next to it and under it, "Star Glyph to remove Parasitic DNA Mutation that invites in entities and is an energetic link to Fear Programming. This glyph restores the DNA. Please circulate widely and reproduce freely -- (Do not Alter) use with integrity. Humans were DNA altered by genetic engineering at the time of the fall of Atlantis and Babylon. A parasitic mutation attached (recessive gene) to DNA making humans susceptible to entities." I have included a copy of this glyph below.

Star Glyph - Restoring Divine DNA Blueprint

There was the name, Judith K. Moore, and her e-mail address on the page. (I later received a reading by Judith Moore which I have posted as Appendix H.) I have always been fascinated by glyphs and this one was certainly no exception. I printed the page and cut out the picture of the glyph. I then thought "All right, what should I do with it?" It said "Use with integrity," but I wondered, how? At that moment I either decided or was guided to place the drawing on my solar plexus. I immediately felt a tremendous amount of activity in my liver. I would call it pain on the level of two on a one to ten scale. Not enough to have me running screaming down the street, but definitely very noticeable. This went on for several minutes, after which I did a little energy healing on the area. I tried this again the next day, but nothing happened. My son, Patrick, tried the glyph in the same manner, but did not notice anything. I wasn't sure what it was all about, but I thought "Whatever it was, I had it, and now it's gone." I also thought "Whoever created this glyph with this much power, I can do that!"

A couple of years before that incident, while I was meditating, I saw a vision of a paper with writing on it. I took that to mean I should try guided writing. The next day I went out on our deck with a notebook and pen in hand. I did my best to clear my mind and started writing whatever thoughts came to me. The first page was just gibberish. On the second page I got, "We are beings of Light and we are here to guide you." What followed was a profound writing from nature spirits. I continued to practice this and find I am now able to readily communicate with unseen benevolent guides as well as our Source. I want to point out that I am a conscious channel and do not go into a trance to receive messages.

Following my introduction to Judith Moore's glyph, I asked my guides how glyphs are created. They gave me a brief review of how this is done. I then set about making some elementary glyphs of my own, with just some simple words: "Energy", "Industriousness", "Joy", and so forth. These efforts achieved no noticeable results. I then decided that to obtain such things as joy, one needed to remove the negative emotional baggage standing in the way.

It was about that time that I received a call from my friend Kathy. She told me that three weeks earlier she had taken her dogs' glass drinking bowl out of the dishwasher while it was still hot, placed it on the floor, and without thinking poured cold water into the bowl. It was like it exploded, she told me, with a piece of glass being driven deep into her foot. Although she was able to remove the glass, the foot was now badly infected, inflamed with considerable swelling, painful, oozing and had a foul odor. Although Kathy is a registered nurse, she knows the importance of avoiding antibiotics unless they are absolutely necessary. Knowing my background in various healing modalities, she asked me if I knew of anything that could help her foot. My first thought was a type of antibiotic herb. But then I decided I would create a glyph and program it to destroy bacteria. I asked Kathy if she would be willing to participate in a little research, to which she agreed. I created two glyphs, one that would take care of the bacteria, and a second glyph to speed healing, then e-mailed them to Kathy. She e-mailed me the following the next day. "I really think my glyphs are working! I put them on upside down on top of my dressing: bacteria killers first and then cell renewal. My foot was swollen, red and oozing to the point where I had to change the bandages at least four or five times a day. This morning, the swelling was way down, the wound look cleaner and there was practically no drainage. Also, it doesn't burn and hurt. Wow!!!" When I spoke to her a couple of weeks later, she said the wound was almost completely healed.

I continued to create glyphs, concentrating on designing them to remove the negative emotions that seem to plague so many of us. All my life I have been troubled with depression and fear. I was sure that removing these disabling energies was an important step in my path. Using myself as a guinea pig, I found that the glyphs easily and effectively began removing more and more of the emotional baggage I had been carrying. Instead of waking up in the morning feeling depressed, I found myself feeling lighter, vibrant and glad to be alive during these exciting times. Being very sensitive to energy, I could feel the glyphs working. I created glyphs to remove heavy metals and other toxic matter safely from the body, with no side effects. Again, I could feel the sensation of something being drawn out of the body.

We are all a part of the energy of our Source. That means within us is all the power we need to heal ourselves and to draw to us everything we desire. Our one failing, however, is that we don't believe we possess that power. All the doubts, fears and negative programming we have accumulated over the years are blocking our way. We may realize this, but that doesn't make these obstacles go away.

These negative beliefs stick to us like glue. There are those who would suggest counseling which has its place, however, it can be expensive, not to mention the time spent sitting in someone's office while they attempt to dredge out all of the deep, dark secrets that go all the way back to before we can remember. Others might suggest past life regression to delve into horrendous lifetimes of pain and torture. Again, this might be helpful but when we stop to realize that we have had hundreds of lifetimes, we can see that may not be a very practical answer. Prayer Glyphs can remove much of whatever is holding us back without digging into painful past memories. Finally we have the tools we need to help heal ourselves. The glyphs in this manual as well as those in Unlocking the Power of Glyphs, will provide the codes and keys for Divine awakening.

The idea of drawings on a piece of paper being so powerful that they can destroy cancer cells or heal a damaged brain may seem difficult to believe. We must think for a moment of the power of the Word, the power of intention and the power of prayer. The amount of energy here is immeasurable by any of our standards. To those who do not believe this is possible, I quote the words of Albert Einstein, *"The most beautiful thing we can experience is the mysterious. It is the source of all true art and science... He who can no longer pause to wonder and stand rapt in awe, is as good as dead; his eyes are closed."*

Sacred Symbols of Light

The glyphs in this manual are a form of spiritual energy. Each glyph invokes a powerful invocation directed at a specific thing for a specific purpose. Direction for these symbols was given to me by Source. I was told to write this book by Source. When I asked Source, "By what name should I call you in the book?" I was told, "By my name, Source Energy, God, Jehovah, Creator or Christ. It is all the same."

These glyphs are energized by highly evolved spiritual beings including Jesus, Mary, Buddha, St. Germain, Quan Yin, the Ascended Masters, Archangels and hundreds more, during a special ceremony at a sacred site high in the Blue Ridge Mountains. The energy from the glyph, together with prayers and intentions of the user, form a strong bond that enhances the body's ability to resolve inner-conflict, release negative patterns and mend old wounds. Every person is an extension of Source Energy and, therefore, is unlimited. As a part of our Source, nothing can prevent us from achieving happiness, health and abundance for ourselves.

Using the Glyphs

When using these glyphs, it is important to focus on gratitude to elevate your vibration which will make you more receptive to healing energies. Every morning, make a list of all the things you are grateful for. Focus on these thoughts and verbally release any negative emotions.

It is important to see ourselves as already free of any illness; thinking about or talking about our perceived problems only serves to re-create negative energy patterns. See yourself the way you want to be; you will be guided in that direction. It is important to recognize that we create our own reality. Every thought creates a flow of energy. We draw to us illness or other problems by negative thinking. In the same manner, we can change that by elevating our thoughts to be more positive. This change in our attitude will create a powerful transformation. Although the glyphs can help us release emotions we are holding within us, they cannot prevent us from accumulating more unless we are willing to make these changes.

The problems that are holding us back are buried deep within us -- like the layers of an onion. You peel-off one layer at a time. This continues until all the layers are removed. Be patient! It may take some time, but work with the glyphs. Sometimes you may feel something happening, especially if you are sensitive to energy. Other times you will not notice anything. That does not mean they are not working -- the energy is subtle. The longer you work with the glyphs, the better results you will achieve. Use a fabric tape or some type of medical tape to hold them in place. Experiment!

Although the energy from the glyphs can move throughout the body, sometimes the best results can be obtained from placing the glyph on the chakra of the area where the problem is located. A picture showing the location of the chakras is included as Appendix B. The glyphs work best when the body is completely relaxed. Most of them can be used anywhere on the body. The emotional-release glyphs will be helpful on all chakras and especially over organs and glands.

We can harbor emotional blockages anywhere, even in our feet and toes. Try putting the glyphs on the bottoms of your feet, where many reflexology and acupuncture meridian points are located. This is best done by covering a shoe insert with a sheet of the glyphs, taping-down the corners, then inserting this into a loose-fitting sock to wear at night. If the sensation is too intense and keeps you from sleeping, remove them and try again another night. The intensity will decrease as negative emotions or toxins are removed from your body. Do not underestimate the importance of an affirmation or prayer. If you have a prayer or affirmation that feels better to you than the one in this manual, by all means say one that you find meaningful to you.

The glyphs can also be used remotely, meaning you can place a page of glyphs on a dresser or bookcase and write your name and where you want to energy to go to in your body. Then INTEND that this be so. Do not doubt that this can work.

For Your Health

Ensure that you drink plenty of water daily -- at least sixty-four ounces. Coffee, tea and carbonated beverages do not count. Carbonated beverages should be avoided completely. To perform at its best, the body needs to be well hydrated. Eat plenty of fresh organic fruits and vegetables which contain oxygen and the Life Force. Avoid the use of sugar and added fructose as they depress the immune system and drain your energy. Also avoid the use of artificial sweeteners; they are toxic to the body and have the adverse effect of causing a craving for carbohydrates. Processed foods are empty calories and processed oils are toxic. Get in the habit of reading labels and seeking out healthy choices. It is all a part of loving yourself and taking good care of your body.

Another important step to remove density is to give up the eating of animal flesh. This keeps people in the lower chakra level. It is important for you to be aware that the need for the consumption of meat has been programmed into you by those who are trying to maintain control over you and your money. There has been a through indoctrination by the establishment that the consumption of meat is essential to our health. This is total fabrication. The medical association that dictates the dissemination of dietary guidelines is part of a large network of organizations that profit in many ways by keeping the population in ignorance and controlling their beliefs. The truth of your body's dietary needs and abilities is that your body is capable of taking anything you consume and using it to produce any nutrient your body requires provided you are able to give up any other controlling beliefs. For that reason it is suggested that you go slowly in changing your diet until you are able to reprogram the belief that your body requires the consumption of meat.

Practice deep-breathing exercises -- a person on a healing path requires plenty of oxygen. The importance of doing breath work cannot be overstated.

Get plenty of exercise -- exercise relieves depression and stimulates digestion. If you hate to exercise, take up dancing or join a hiking club.

Release judgment. We hold our judgements within us, which will prevent us from healing. The one we judge most often is our self. It is important that we not be so hard on ourselves. Love yourself, warts and all! It is also important to love unconditionally. We find that to be most difficult when dealing with those we are with most often. We place expectations upon them, feeling they should live up to those expectations. Again, the one we have the most difficulty loving unconditionally is our own self – then how can we love others if we don't love ourselves? Learn to practice acceptance when we are in a situation we cannot change. We don't make mistakes, we don't do things wrong; we learn from our life experiences. Remember, each of us is on our own spiritual path and we all have the right to make our own choices. We don't need to concern ourselves with the choices that others make; we have no way of knowing what their path is.

I am often asked "Do you have to believe in the power of the glyphs in order for them to work?" The glyphs work very well on our pets. Animals do not think, "Will this work?" "Is this possible?" "Why don't I feel anything?" They neither believe nor disbelieve, they just are. When a person puts their intent into any healing modality, it makes the healing potential that much stronger. However, when one is doubtful or a skeptic, it puts out a negative energy that prevents the full impact of the glyph to do its work. Worry is also a negative energy that can interfere with any healing modality. I strongly discourage anyone from trying to talk another person into using these glyphs. A willing and positive person will benefit a great deal while the skeptic may be just as determined to prove the glyphs do not work. The glyphs can be used remotely on other persons with the approval of their soul but the glyphs cannot overcome free will. Some people who are very attached to their negativity or illness will choose to judge and criticize rather than trying something new and it is best to just leave them be.

When working with pets, tape the glyph on the chakras of an animal's back when they are sleeping. Use a tape that can easily be removed. A picture showing chakra locations on a dog is included in Appendix A. The chakras for cats can be found in the same locations. Glyphs can also be used remotely on pets and in some cases with long haired animals, it may be the only way possible.

There are several glyphs in this manual that are designed to restore surgically removed organs or glands. You may ask, "Is this possible?" Remember, as a part of Source energy, anything is possible. The only limitation you have is in your mind. The glyphs give the direction of using stem cells and bone marrow to restore the body part. You must give up the idea that this is not possible. How long it takes is up to you and how effective you are in changing your beliefs.

As in Book I, the numbering of the glyphs is not consecutive. This is because many of the glyphs were created for specific persons who had specific problems. Other glyphs were not appropriate for listing in this manual.

Using the Glyphs

The following pages contain a title and explanation page for each glyph followed by a patch page of the glyph that you will want to copy for personal use of the purchaser of this manual and his/her family. These glyphs can be used in several ways:

- As a whole page to place the hands on (very powerful while sleeping or lying down).

- As a block of four or nine to place under the back of heart chakra while sleeping. (This may also cover the back of the solar plexus.)

- Cut with a scissors to fit a shoe insert for placing in a large bootie or sock to be worn while sleeping.

- Cut out individually and taped over a chakra.

- Cut out in a block of four to be used over a chakra (to be sure you cover the location).

- If this is an eBook, the glyphs can be used as an iron on transfer on cloth. These transfers can be purchased at your local office supply store. Follow the instructions carefully. If you damage them, they will not work.

- When glyphs are cut out, include the black border (I do not mean the dotted line).

- If the glyph becomes wet or damaged in any way, discard it.

Take a block of 9, 12 or 16 glyphs (the size of your hand) and put them by your bedside when you go to sleep. When you first start to wake up, take the glyphs and hold them between your palms, while lying on your side or when lying on your back, hold them over your solar plexus with both hands on the glyphs for 10 or 15 minutes or as long as you have time.

The glyphs can also be used remotely, meaning you can place a glyph or page of glyphs on a dresser or bookcase, write your name on a piece of paper and write where you want energy to be directed to in your body. Then INTEND that this be so. Do not doubt that this is possible. Believe in your power through intention.

It is helpful to say the affirmation out loud, as the words have a positive vibration to them that will be very helpful.

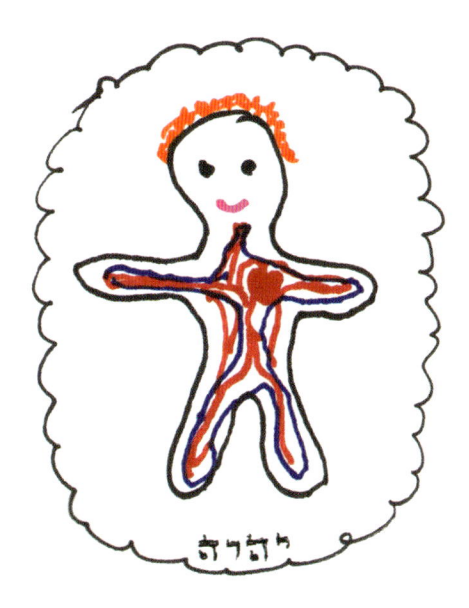

Glyph 11 - Circulatory System

This glyph is empowered to restore strength and elasticity to capillaries, veins, blood vessels, heart and other circulatory parts. It can also remove blockages and constrictions. Used consistently it removes plaque from the heart, arteries or other parts of the circulatory system. Continued use can help vein problems as well as. Be sure to use *glyphs #2, #5, #6, and #82* from Book I to resolve emotional causes of circulatory problems. These unresolved emotions are at the root of vein problems along with feeling burdened. Practice gratitude and learn to "Love What Is."

Ways to use this glyph:

Use on the back of heart, the back of the solar plexus and/or under your feet while you sleep. If you feel guided to use in another location, do so. For long standing vein problems, use remotely. It is also important to be using the *Detox Glyphs #4, 44 and Chakra Glyph #9*.

Suggested Affirmation:
I am strong and healthy, perfect the way I am. I hold the thought of joy and gratitude for all my many blessings. I intend health and wellness for every day.

Glyph 11 - Circulatory System

Glyph 12 - Urethra and Bladder

Regular use of this glyph will help restore elasticity to the bladder, supporting muscles and tissues and to restore elasticity and strength to the urethra. Following a healthy diet and regular exercise will also be important. You will need to let go of anxiety and holding on to old ideas. Use the glyphs from Book I for overcoming fear.

Ways to use this glyph:

Use this glyph on the solar plexus, sacral chakra and/or remotely. Use under the bottom of the feet.

Suggested Affirmation:

I release all anger and resentment that I have held within me. I realize that I am responsible for my own reality and there is no one to blame for anything that happens in my life. I understand that to make changes in my life, I must change.

Glyph 12 - Urethra and Bladder

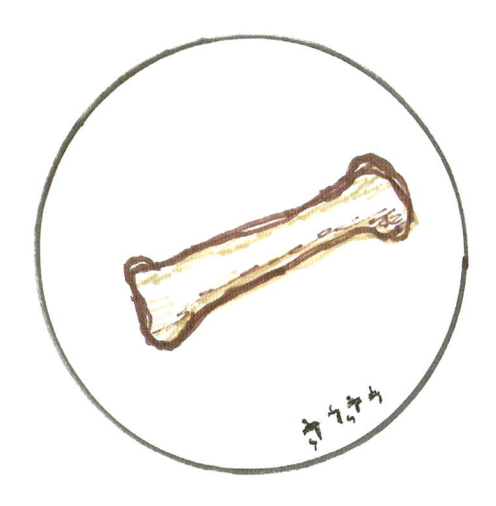

Glyph 20 - Bones and Cartilage

This glyph can help with many types of bone problems including thinning, diseased and injured bones. It can also help with joint problems. Be sure to use glyphs from Book I to resolve emotional issues that are the cause of bone problems. See yourself as well and let go of the past. This is a powerful glyph.

Ways to use this glyph:

Cut out a block of glyphs, tape them to a shoe insert and put inside a loose booty to wear at night. To resolve degeneration, do this often and also use remotely. Proper alkaline diet and exercise are important.

Take a block of 9, 12 or 16 (the size of your hand) glyphs and put them by your bedside when you go to sleep. When you first start to wake up, take the glyphs and hold them between your palms, while lying on your side, under or in front of your face and relax completely for 10 or 15 minutes.

Tape a glyph (or a small block of glyphs) over the part of your body that needs help. This can be worn in the daytime but is especially helpful at night. Go with whatever guidance you receive. This glyph really helped my dog's arthritis. Use remotely.

Suggested Affirmation:
I am a pillar of Light as I stand tall in God's creation.
I honor myself as a part of God. I am grateful and I bless myself as I bless others.

Glyph 20 - Bones and Cartilage

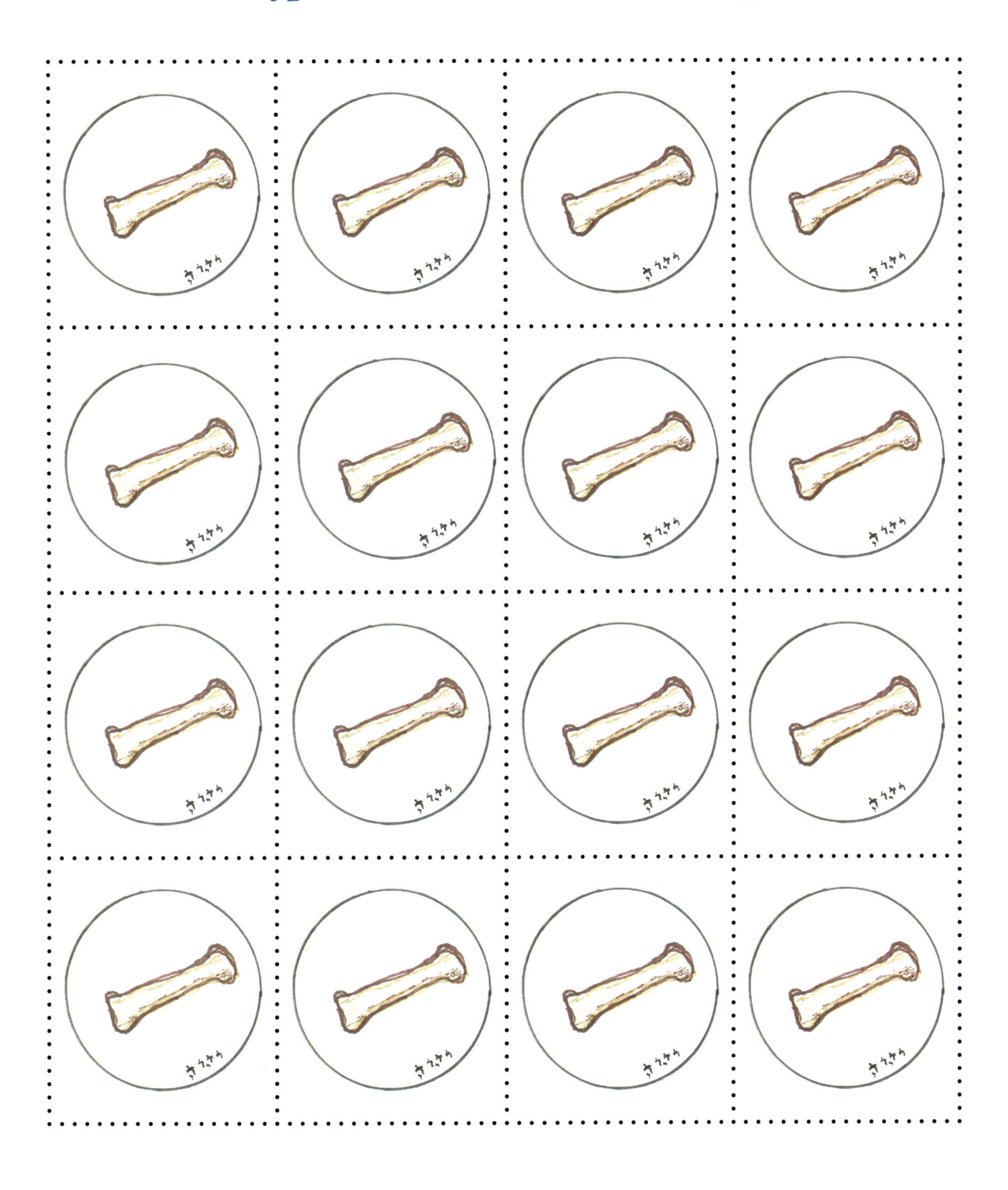

27

Glyph 21 - Pituitary, Thalamus, Hypothalamus and Pineal

This glyph can modify the DNA of the pituitary, thalamus, hypothalamus and pineal to the original blueprint, remove the death hormone, and provide regeneration and detoxification of the same. This glyph will also harmonize and balance the nervous system, the endocrine system and biochemistry of the body. Understand that the death hormone and the DNA are under the influence of your beliefs and attitude. A belief in dying will prevail so it is important to give up the programming that "everyone must die sometime." Remember, you are Source energy and the only limitation you have is that which you place upon yourself. Be sure and use the emotional release glyphs from Book I.

Ways to use this glyph:

Use this glyph on the crown chakra and/or the third eye or whatever you feel guided to use it.

> ### Suggested Affirmation:
> I release any idea that I am aging. I see myself in total perfect health.
> I accept responsibility for everything that is in my life at this time
> and I see only good coming to me now.

Glyph 21 - Pituitary, Thalamus, Hypothalamus and Pineal

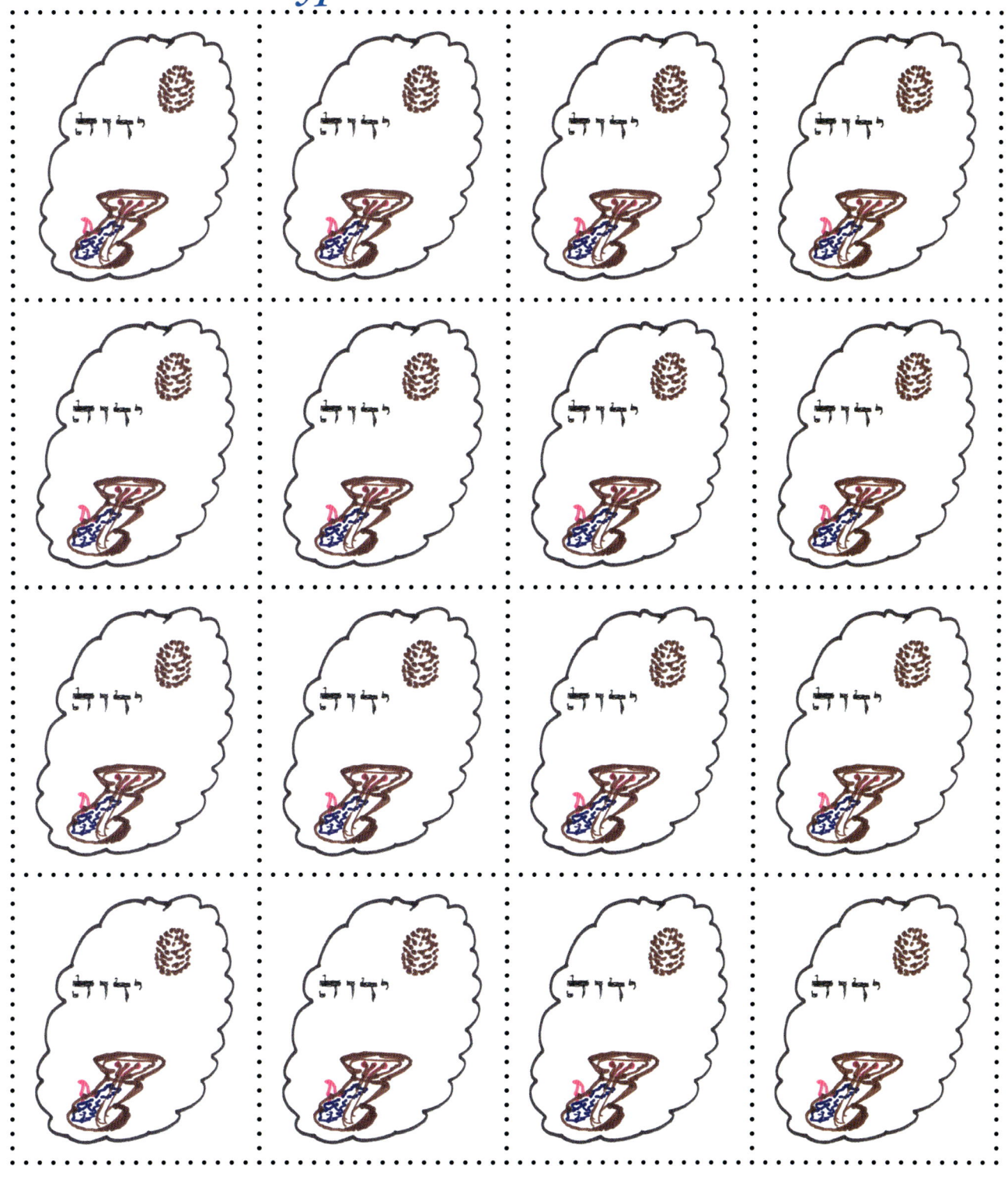

Glyph 28 - Vaccinations

This glyph will remove any traces of any type of vaccinations in the past, present or beyond that are not for the highest good of the individual and in total harmony with the body. It can also repair damage done by the offending vaccination. The time it takes for this to resolve problems resulting from vaccinations will depend on the receptivity of the individual and the amount of damage that must be repaired.

Ways to use this glyph:

Take a block of these glyphs and hold them between your hands when going to sleep. Also use them at night on your feet. Use remotely to work on extensive damage repair.

Suggested Affirmation:
I see myself as perfect in all ways. I understand that I am a part of Source energy and I am unlimited. I see myself free of any toxic or inhibiting matter.

Glyph 28 - Vaccinations

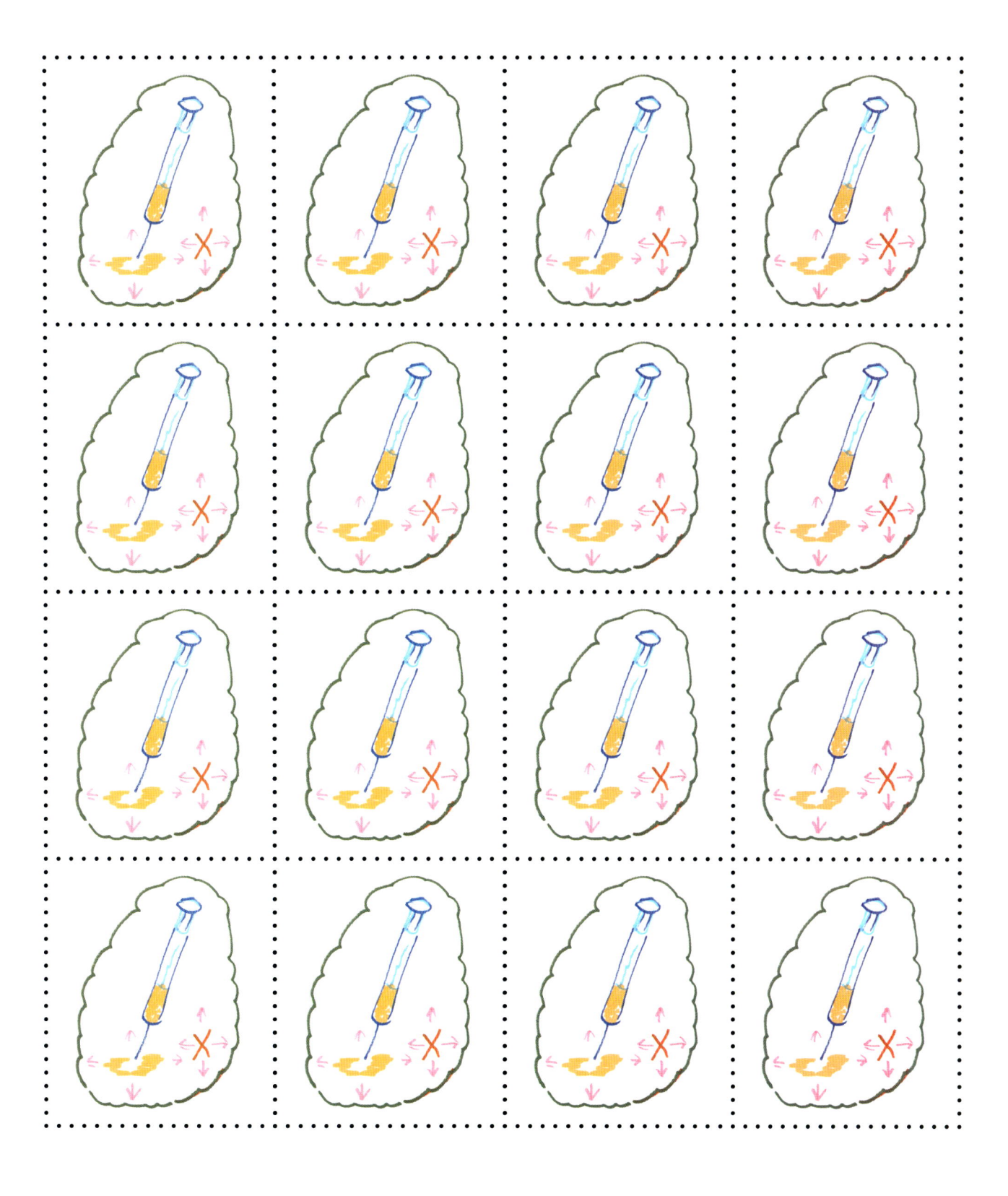

Glyph 31 - Vertebrae Support

Used consistently this glyph can help with many vertebra problems including slipped disk, curvature of the spine and many others. One person stated it helped his slipped disk overnight. Resolving bone curvature can take longer depending upon your ability to overcome seeing yourself with a problem and starting to believe in what you previously thought impossible. Be sure and use all the glyphs removing the emotional problems that are the cause and resolve to see yourself as healed. If you see yourself with a problem, that is what your mind will keep recreating.

Ways to use this glyph:

Use on the solar plexus or over the part of the spine that needs help. This will work even faster when combined with *Glyph #20 - Bones*. Continue by using this glyph remotely and with positive visualization.

Suggested Affirmation:

Creator, as I stand tall in your Light, I ask to be guided to release all of the emotions that stand in the way of my healing. I forgive myself for all of the judgements and denials that have kept me from being close to you.
Thank you God for your Love and Light.

Glyph 31 - Vertebrae Support

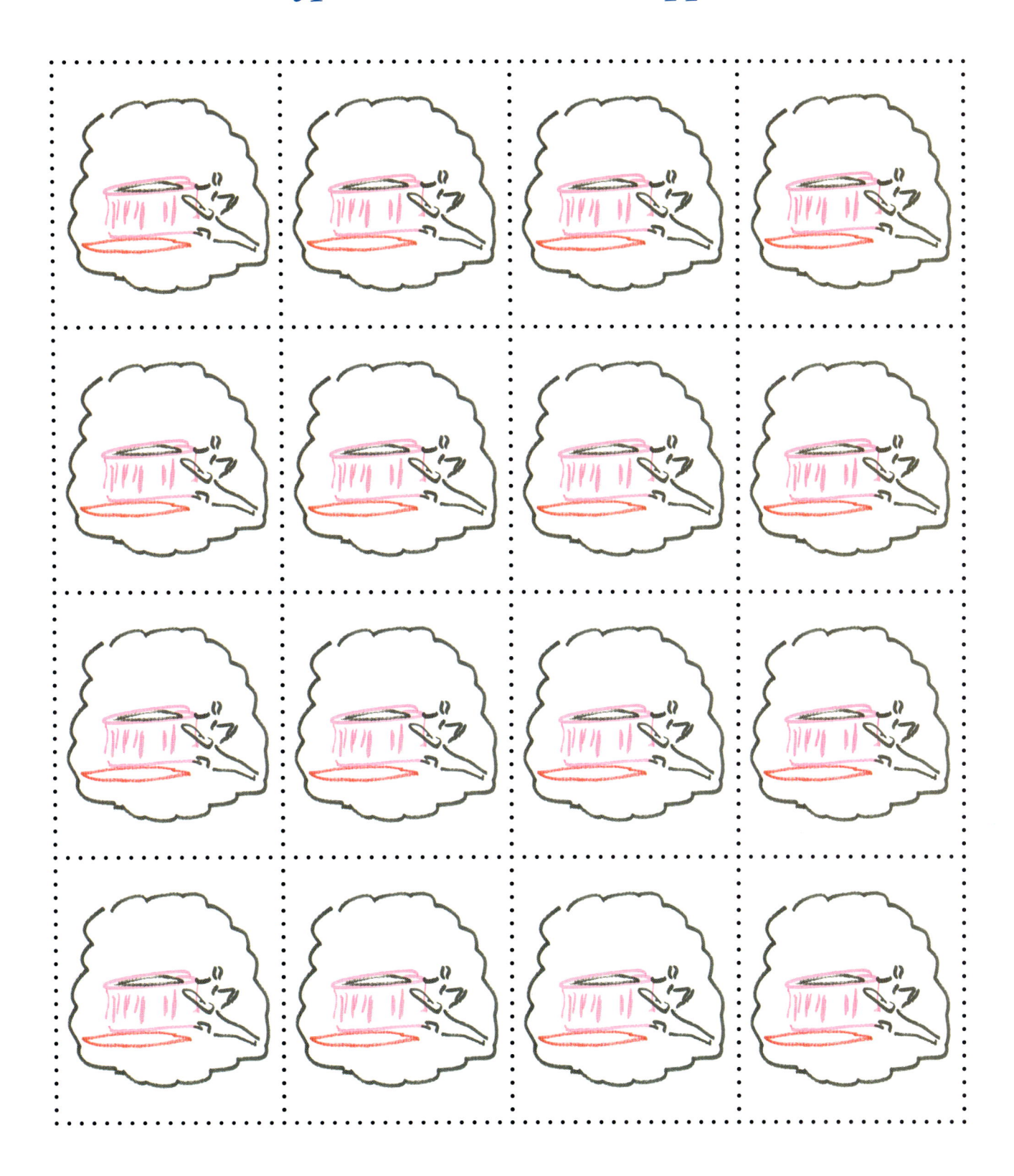

Glyph 32 - Stomach, Liver Gallbladder and Pancreas

This glyph can rebuild the stomach, liver, gallbladder and pancreas by replacing the DNA of all four organs with the DNA of the perfect blueprint. It can also clear these organs of any associated blockages. It is imperative that you think of yourself as well and perfect. If you see yourself as sick or any of these organs as diseased, the DNA will revert back to the sickness. You control your DNA with your mind. For congested liver and gallbladder, consider a gallbladder flush. A healthy diet is imperative.

Ways to use this glyph:

Place this glyph on the solar plexus and under the rib cage on the right side. Leave on overnight and use often. To resolve long term problems, use remotely.

Suggested Affirmation:
I let go of all my fears and trust in the Universe to take care of me.
I am perfect in all ways and I love my body.

Glyph 32 - Stomach, Liver Gallbladder and Pancreas

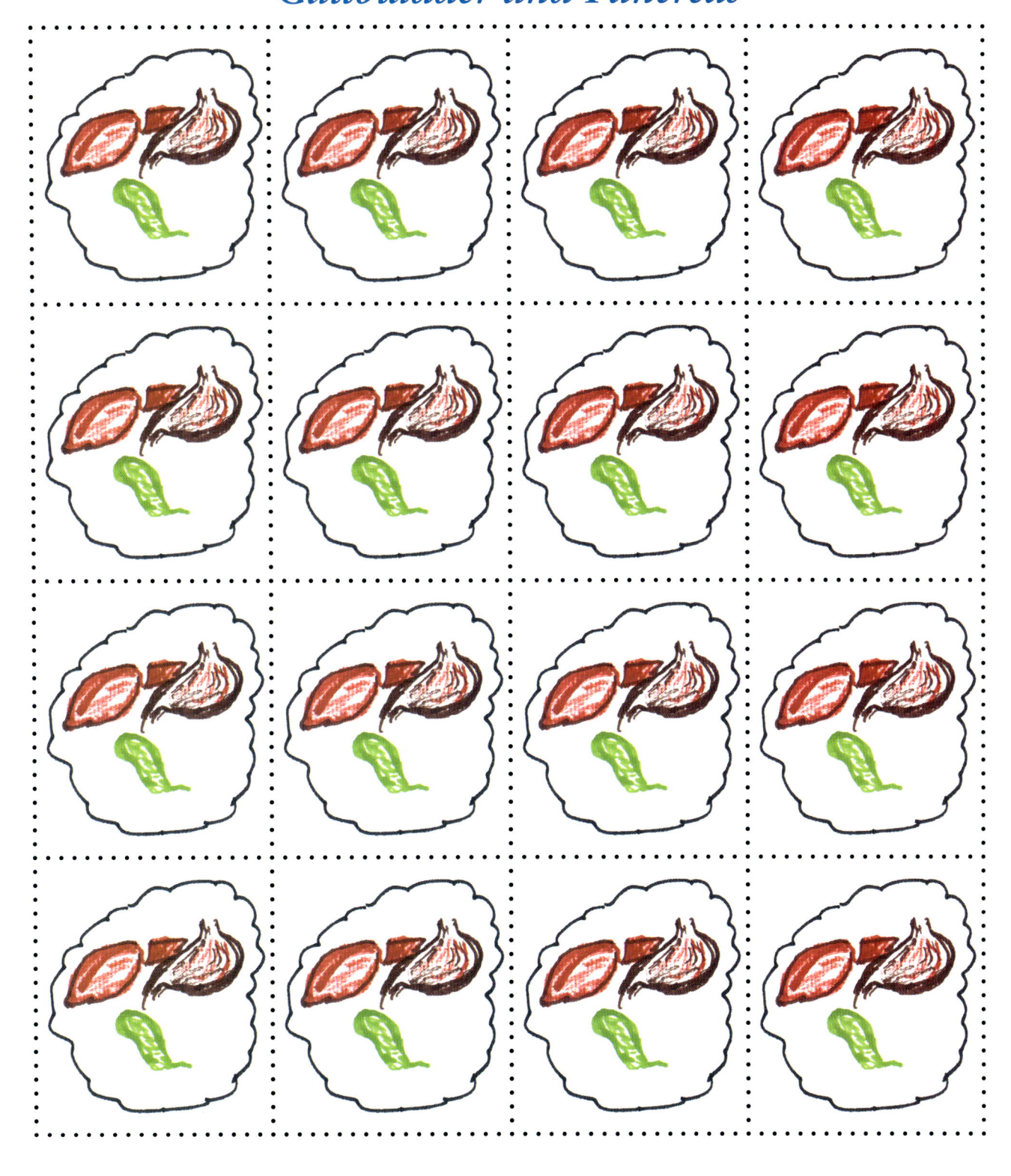

Glyph 33 - Adrenal Glands and Kidneys

Stress and the many toxins in our body have a very damaging effect on our adrenal glands. This glyph can detoxify, rebuild and energize the adrenals. It will also work on cleansing our kidneys and used consistently will break down and remove kidney stones. The glyph is also programmed to regenerate a kidney if one has been removed. This would require belief in ones ability as a connection to Source and positive continual visualization. Read part on page 13 regarding regenerating body parts.

Ways to use this glyph:

Use on the minor chakra on the back of the navel. Use remotely for extensive work removing stones or rebuilding.

Suggested Affirmation:

I see myself as perfect in every way. I trust creation and the universe to provide all my needs. I realize there is never any need for worry or concern over anything. Everything is in Divine order

Glyph 33 - Adrenal Glands and Kidneys

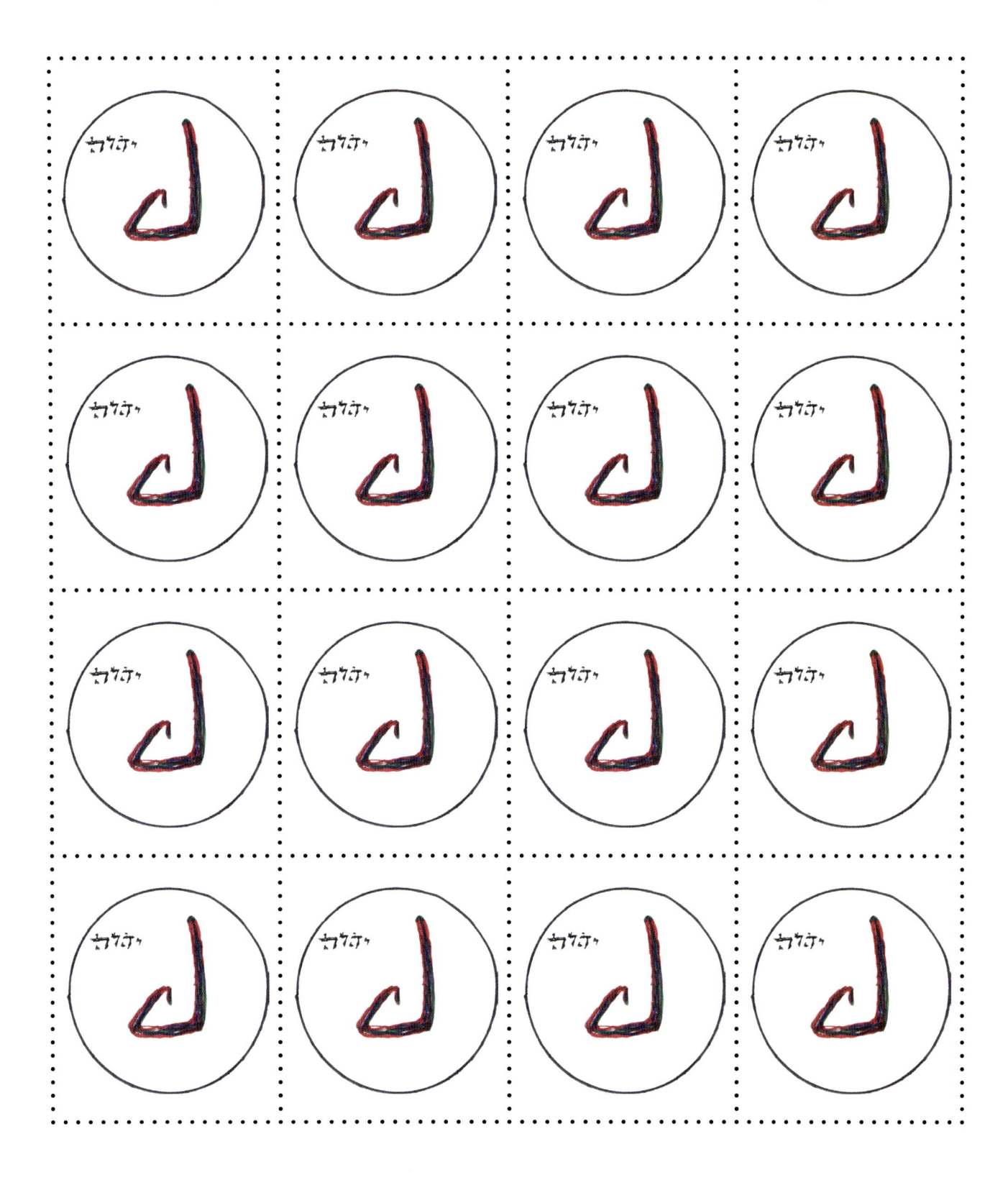

Glyph 34 - Clear Vision

This glyph is programmed to resolve a great number of eye problems including cataracts, glaucoma, macular degeneration, retina problems and more. Be sure and use all the glyphs from the book removing the emotional and karmic problems that are the cause and avoid thinking of yourself as having this problem. This glyph completely resolved cataracts for my former husband Dean as well as his glaucoma.

Ways to use this glyph:

Using soft medical tape, place one of these glyphs over the eyes while sleeping, tape one on each side of the lower back of the head at the indentation where the skull meets the neck (this location is very important for glaucoma). Put one on the ajna chakra (between the eyebrows). I also received a message that one should be put under each arm (armpit) which we did only once, and one just above the elbow joint on the outside (we did not do this but had success anyway). Put one where ever you feel guided to do so and use remotely. Use this remotely on pets with eye problems.

Suggested Affirmation:

Creator, help me to clear my vision so that I may understand and see my mission. Give me the clarity and the wisdom to follow the Divine Plan. Open my eyes that I may see with love and understanding. Let me see only the good in others so that they will see only the good in me.

Glyph 34 - Clear Vision

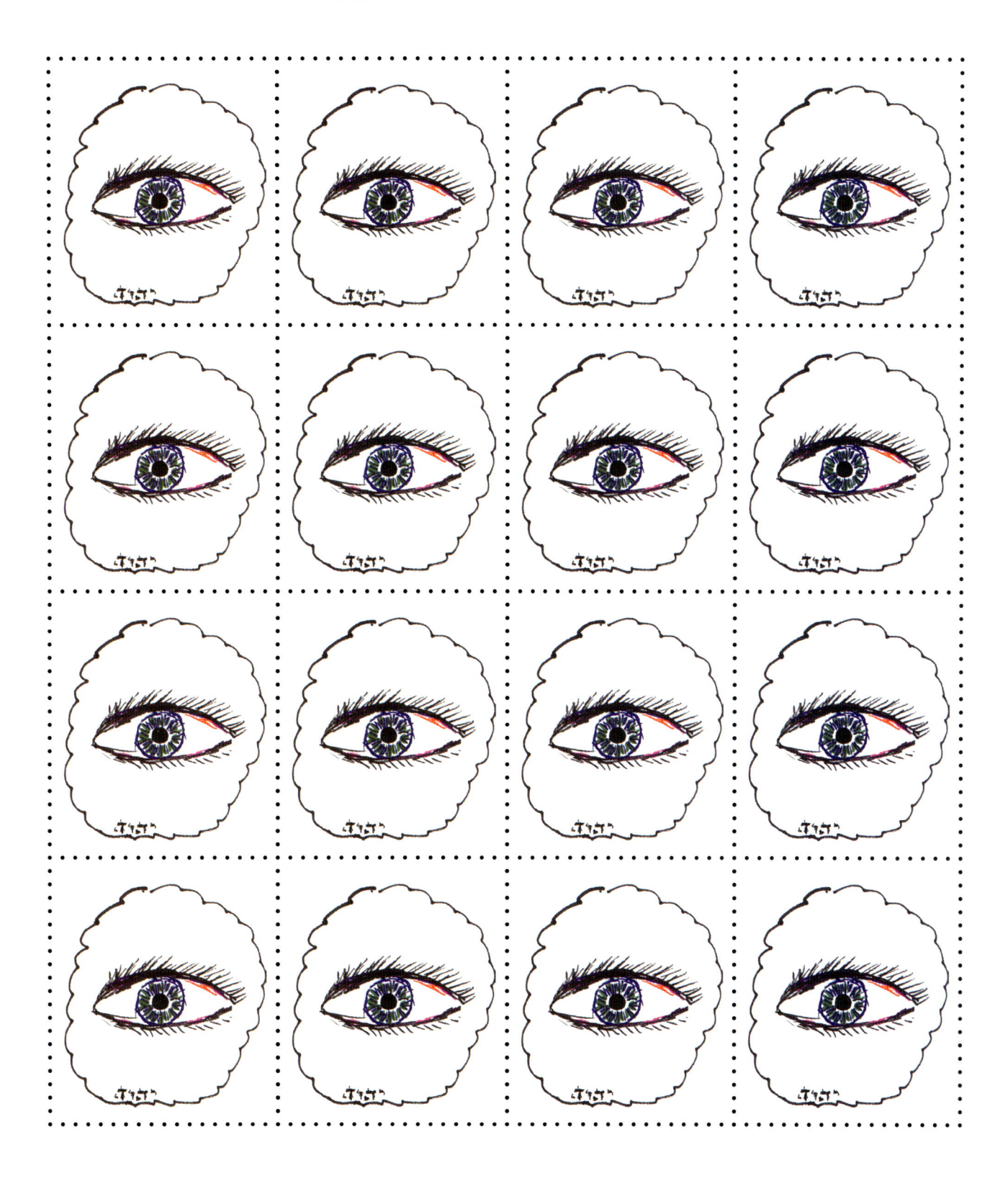

Glyph 35 - Hearing/Ear/Olfactory

This glyph can help resolve some hearing problems. It can restore the DNA representing parts of the body associated with hearing including the ear drum, all parts of the middle ear and inner ear. It can help remove emotional blockages to hearing and repair any damaged, deformed or age-related degenerated parts including the nerves that are causing any loss of hearing. Be sure and use emotional release glyphs in Book I. Long-standing problems can take much longer to resolve. Over time this glyph can also help resolve the loss of the sense of smell.

Ways to use this glyph:

Tape this glyph on the secondary chakra just under the ear and anywhere you feel guided to use it. Also use remotely.

Suggested Affirmation:
I hear the voice of God and it is music to my ears.
May I bask in the glory of the energy that flows though me from my Creator.

Glyph 35 - Hearing/Ear

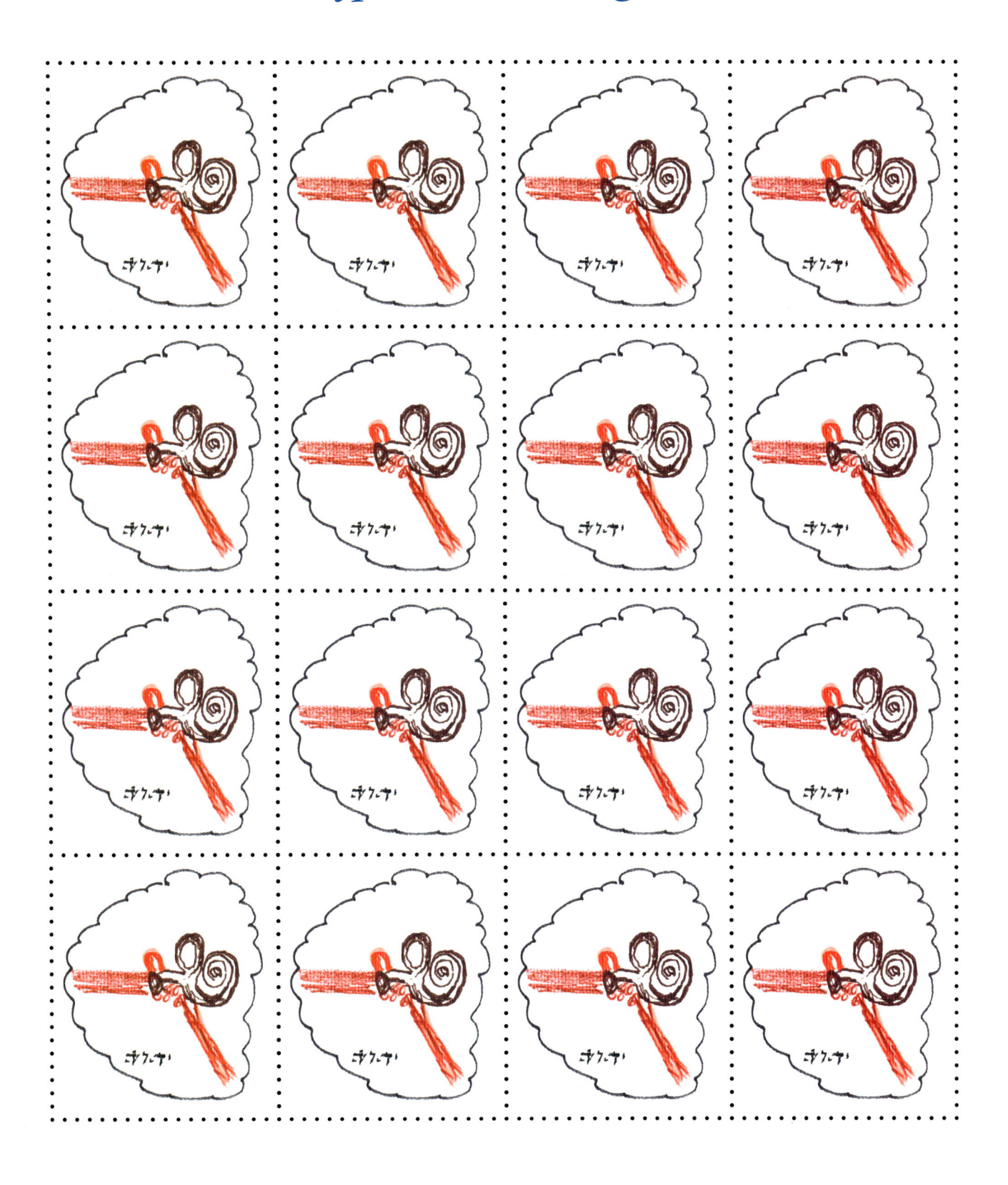

Glyph 36 - Spleen

This glyph can heal and regenerate the spleen. If the spleen has been surgically removed, this glyph has been programmed to restore the spleen utilizing any needed stem cells and bone marrow plus any other needed frequencies with direction to restore function of spleen as it is being regenerated. For an existing spleen it can restore all of the genes from the DNA representing the spleen with the DNA of a healthy spleen. It will balance the body chemistry and hormone levels as needed during this process as well as balance the energies of the right and left hemisphere of the brain. It will also resolve any problem with parasites, virus, bacteria and toxic matter in the spleen. Keep in mind you must work on the emotional issues that affect the spleen. Obsessions are most often the cause of spleen problems.

Ways to use this glyph:

This glyph can be placed on the spleen chakra (under the left rib cage) and solar plexus. After using it a few times directly on the body, it can be used remotely for rebuilding the spleen.

Suggested Affirmation:
I am willing to let go of the desire to control things. I understand that I am here to evolve. I am perfect in every way and I release all that does not serve me. I choose in my life only that which is the highest good.

Glyph 36 - Spleen

59

Glyph 37 – Healing the Heart

Continued use of this glyph can repair and regenerate the heart including all ducts and valves, the aorta and all associated arteries and veins. This may take weeks and even months depending on the situation. For small children, infants and animals, it may work very quickly. It can also clear the heart and arteries of plaque.

Please understand that this glyph is for you as an active participant and not your elderly friends and loved ones who are near the end of their journey. If it is for an infant or child in your care, ask permission of their soul or state the intention. *"I intend this glyph heal this infant/child (Name) if it is for their highest good and in keeping with their soul's journey."* Whatever happens is what is right for their path.

Ways to use this glyph:

Place this glyph or a block of several of these glyphs on the back of the heart chakra. For maximum healing, use for as long as you feel guided to do so. Also use remotely. This glyph healed my heart problem in several weeks.

Suggested Affirmation:
Creator, I give you my heart. Help me to heal myself of any of my perceived weaknesses. My love for you is all I have in my heart.
Help me to understand how I can be of service.

Glyph 37 – Healing the Heart

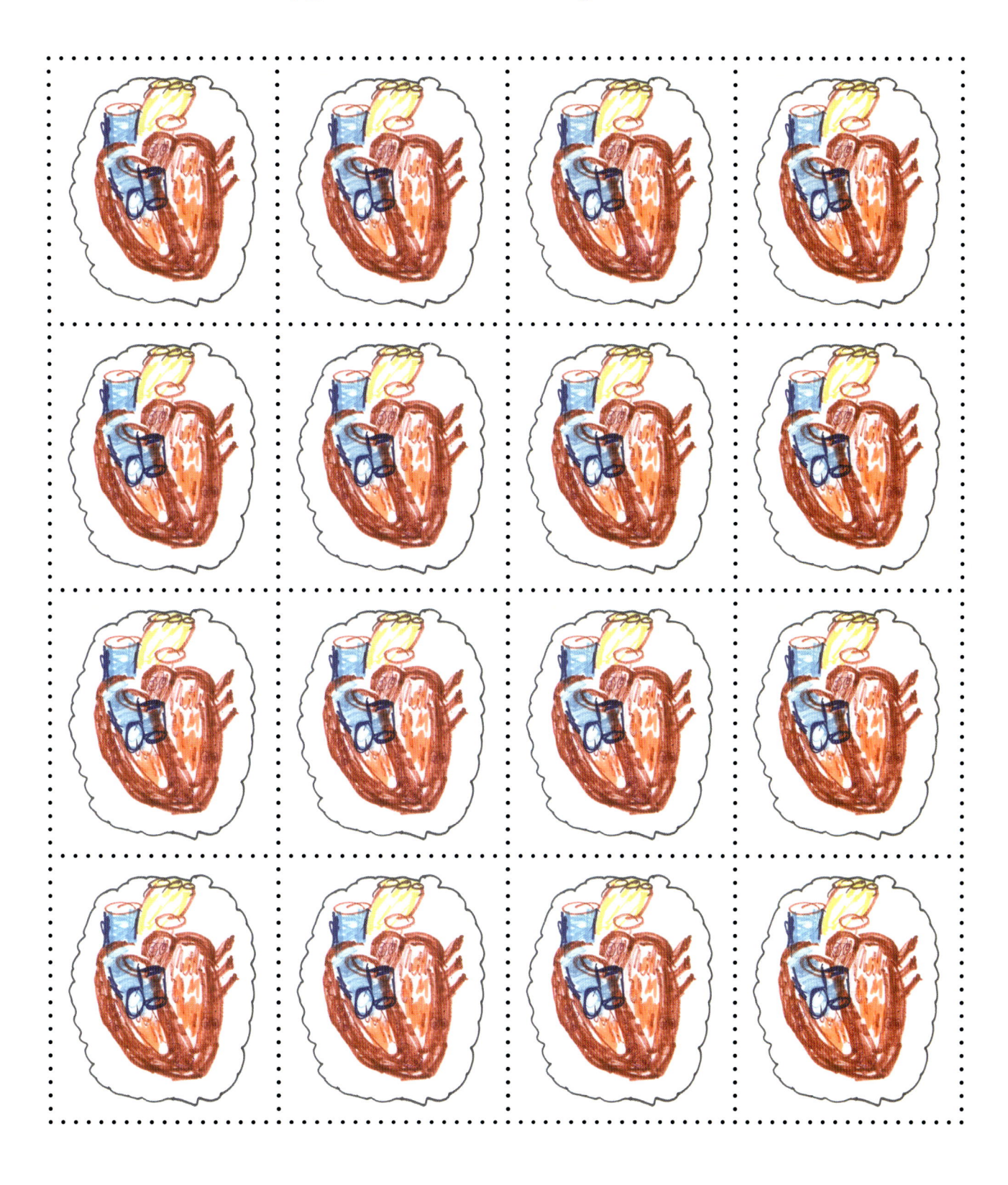

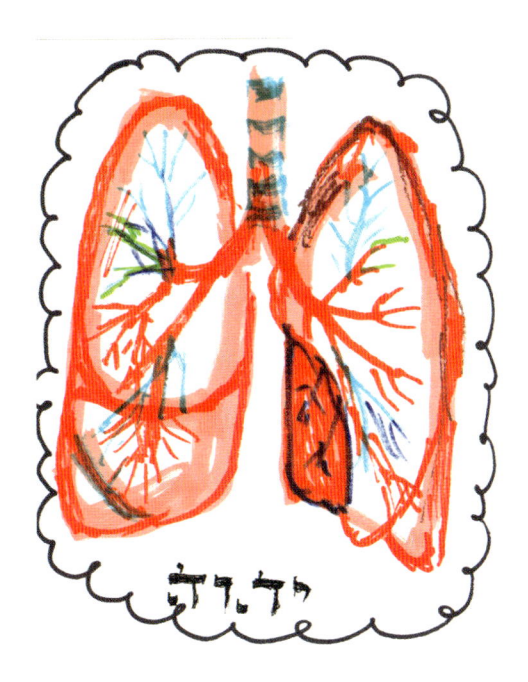

Glyph 38 – Healing the Lungs

Used consistently this glyph can regenerate the lungs, all associated valves and damaged lung tissue. It can also remove any emotional blockages from the lungs and trachea and transition to Light any toxic matter, bacteria, viruses, yeast or other fungi from the lungs including any die-off.

Ways to use this glyph:

Place this glyph or a block of several of these glyphs on the back of the heart chakra. The time it takes to heal serious lung problems will depend on the user. This glyph can be used remotely.

Suggested Affirmation:

With my every breath, my intention is to fulfill why I have come here.
I am grateful for this opportunity to learn from this journey.
I am filled with Light and love all of my days.

Glyph 38 – Healing the Lungs

Glyph 39 - Female Reproductive System

The purpose of this glyph is to restore to health the female reproductive system in the body and the aura. In addition to removing emotional blockages and resolving disease, this glyph is programmed to restore surgically removed parts using any stem cells, bone marrow and other frequencies needed. Is such a thing possible? If you have to ask, maybe not for you. Please read the part about restoring surgically removed organs. CAUTION: If you have past menopause, this glyph may start you ovulating again. Please take precautions if you notice any sign of restored menses.

Ways to use this glyph:

Use on solar plexus, sacral chakra and any other major chakra as you feel guided. Continue to use remotely with your most powerful intention to restore extensive damage.

Suggested Affirmation:
I love my body and feel the creative force of God flowing through me.
I am perfect the way I am and am very grateful for all things in my life.

Glyph 39 - Female Reproductive System

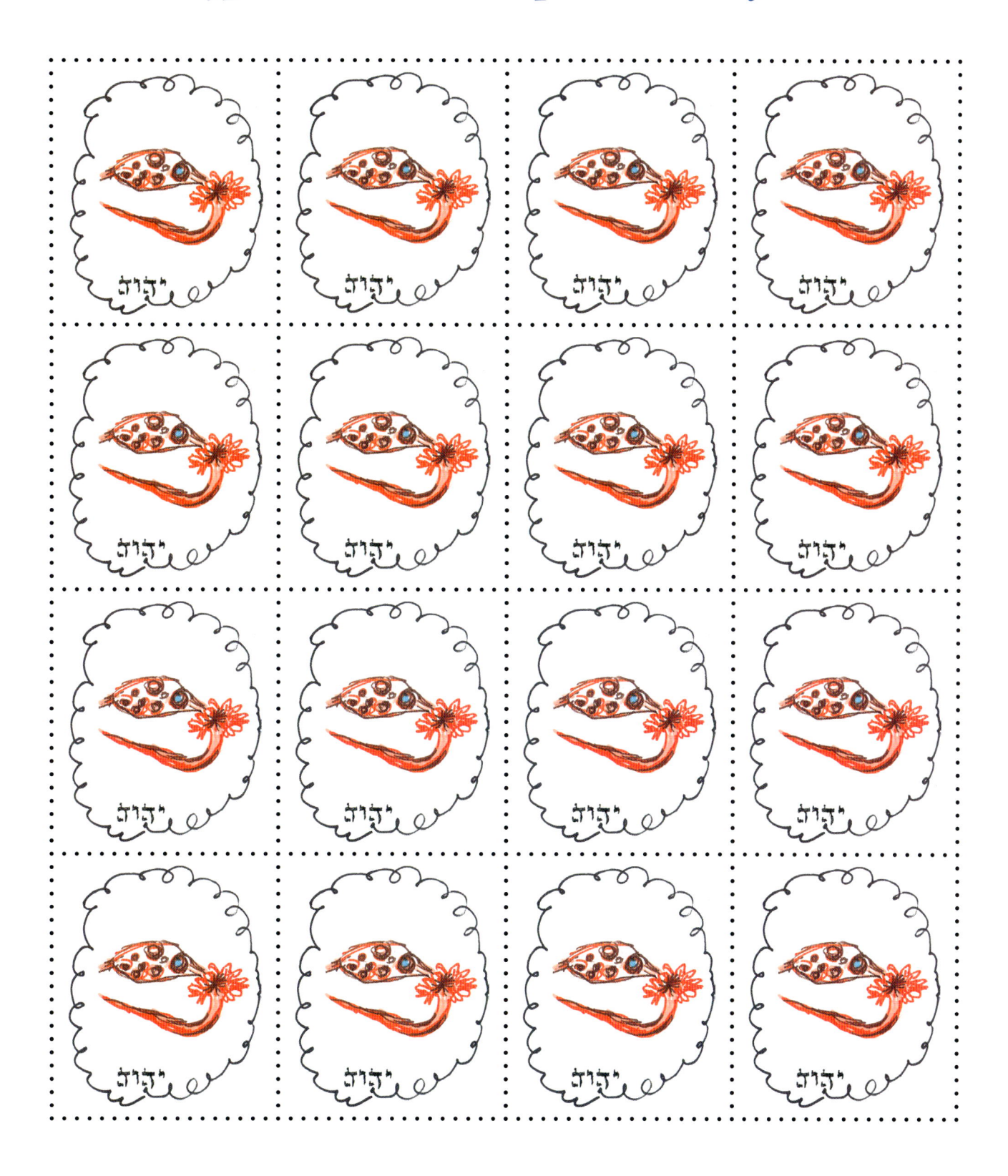

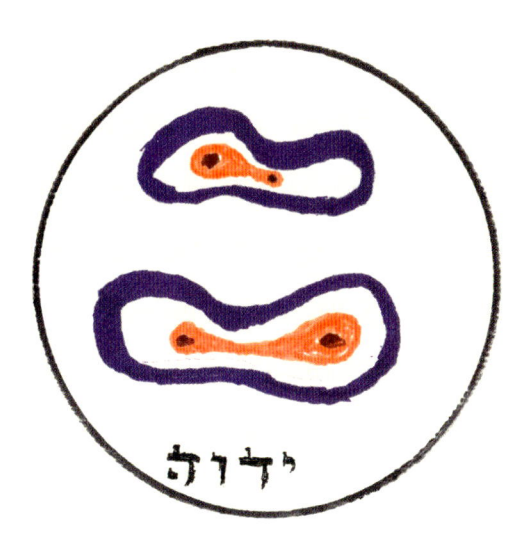

Glyph 40 - Restore Surgically Removed Adenoids

This glyph is designed to restore surgically removed adenoids utilizing any needed stem cells and bone marrow plus any other needed frequencies to restore the function of the adenoids as they are being regenerated. It will also balance body chemistry and hormone levels as needed during this process plus balance the energies of the right and left hemisphere of the brain bringing the user into real time. This glyph will incorporate all intrinsic cellular systems to adjust to new frequencies.

Ways to use this glyph:

The glyph should be placed on the solar plexus, heart chakra, held between the hands or put under the feet while sleeping. After a few days place a sheet of these glyphs in a secure place, on a bookcase or table with a sheet of paper instructing the glyph to continue sending the direction and energy of the glyph to all major chakras of the body of (your name). Place your intent and belief in the ability of this to work. See in your mind's eye that this work is complete.

Suggested Affirmation:

With God's helpful loving hand I am whole and complete.
I see the energy flowing through me with ease. I see myself as healthy and full of energy. I am grateful for the Divine energy that is flowing through me now.

Glyph 40 - Restore Surgically Removed Adenoids

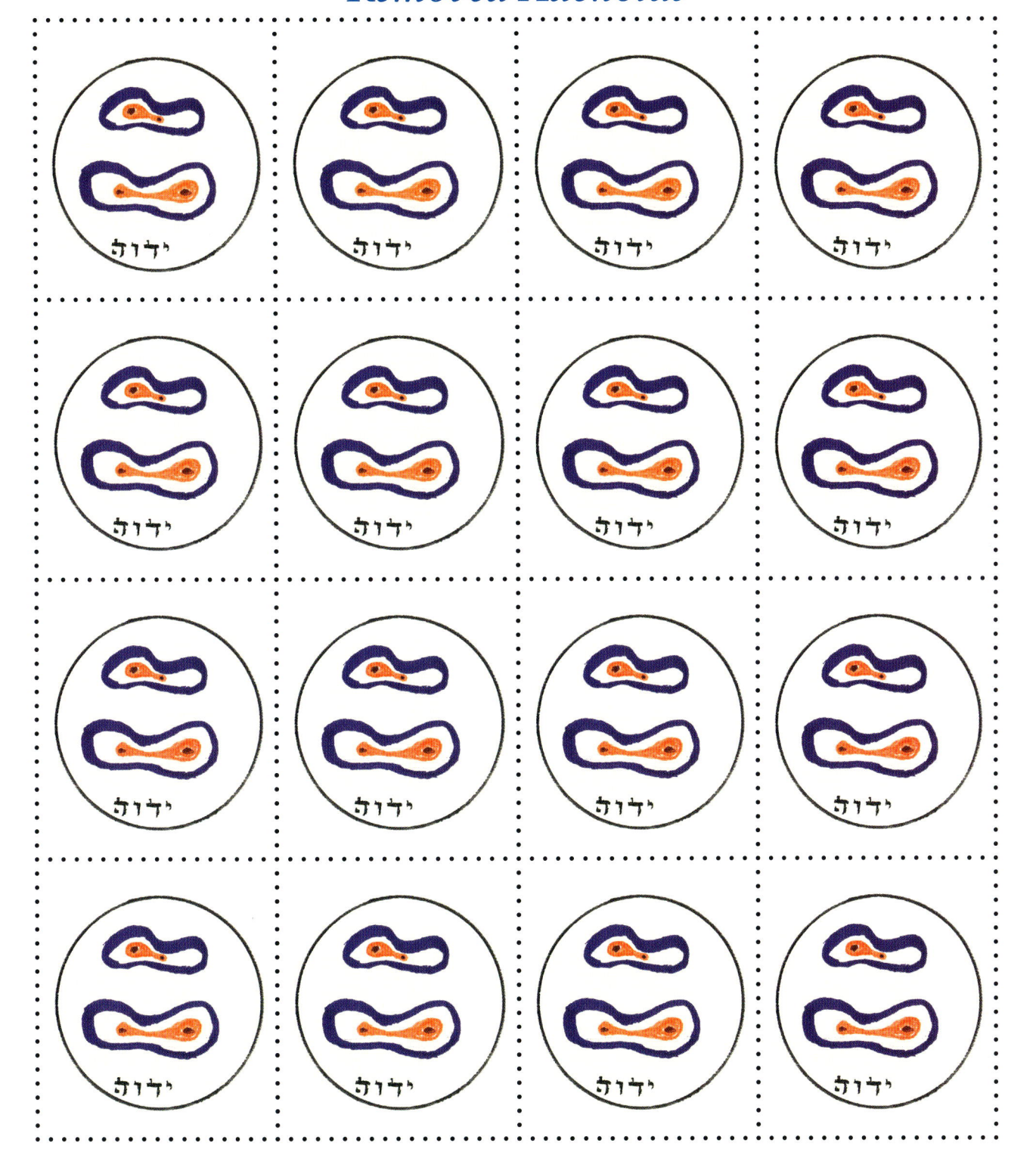

Glyph 41 – Muscle Restoration

The glyph can help repair or regenerate damaged muscles and connecting tissues in the body including muscle lost from wasting diseases. It can also transmute into Light any existing toxic matter found in the muscles and remove emotional blockages associated with the muscular system. Be sure to use the glyphs in Book I resolving emotional causes of muscle problems. This glyph needs to be combined with adequate muscle building exercise.

Ways to use this glyph:

Use this glyph on any major chakra, bottoms of feet or anywhere you feel guided to use it. Also use remotely to resolve long standing muscle damage.

Suggested Affirmation:
I feel the strength and power of the Light running though me now.
I love who I am and move forward with courage and conviction.
I shine my Light proudly.

Glyph 41 – Muscle Restoration

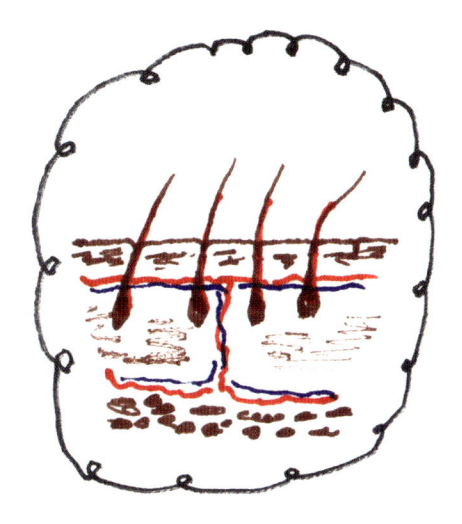

Glyph 43 - Skin Restoration

This glyph can assist in the restoration of the skin. Used consistently it can remove scars and other damage or deformities to the skin including age related anomalies. Given time it can restore lost hair follicles if the cause is resolved, which is fear, tension and the desire to control things.

Ways to use this glyph:

Use on the solar plexus, under the feet, between the hands or any way you feel guided to use it.

Suggested Affirmation:
Creator, I realize that as I am a part of you, I am unlimited.
I ask guidance for all ways that I may use the powers of creation for the highest good. I honor myself and all others and hold them in the Light.

Glyph 43 – Skin Restoration

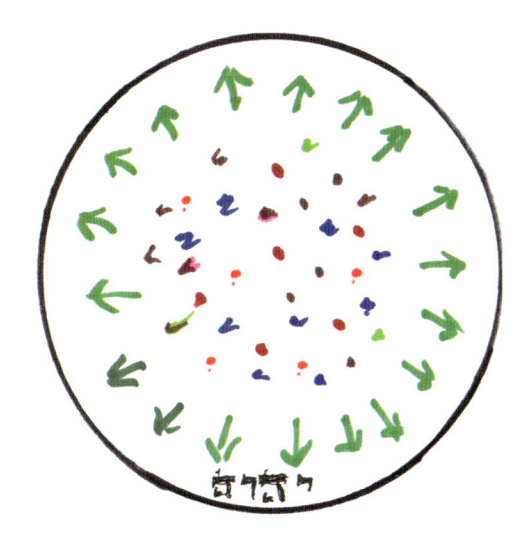

Glyph 44 - Detoxification II

The purpose of this glyph is to remove from the body any heavy metals, pesticides, herbicides, monosodium glutamate, fluoride and any other chemical toxins. It can further transition to Light all acidic wastes and toxic matter that is discharged from parasites or fungus, calcium deposits, kidney stones and bone spurs. It will also remove plaque from the circulatory system.

Ways to use this glyph:

Place on solar plexus, any major chakra, over organ or gland or point of distress. Make print of patches on transfer to iron on white woven fabric, cut to fit and tape to shoe inserts, slip insert inside of loose knit booty to wear while sleeping and use on back of neck. Make transfers to iron on for other items as needed. This glyph can also be used remotely. Use the glyph extensively.

Suggested Affirmation:

Creator, with your help and guidance I release myself from any
toxic matter or debris that is affecting my health or my journey to evolve.
I see myself as a temple of your Light and choose a path of wellness.

Glyph 44 - Detoxification II

Glyph 45 - Male Reproductive System

This glyph can heal and restore the male reproductive system. It is also programmed to rebuild any parts of the male reproductive system that have been surgically removed using any stem cells, bone marrow or any frequencies needed, restoring all male reproductive parts to the original blueprint (see page 11 regarding the regeneration of surgically removed parts) removing any existing toxins, disease or emotional blockages. The glyph can then balance biochemistry and the entire endocrine system.

Ways to use this glyph:

Use on the solar plexus and sacral chakra and any other major chakra you feel guided to use it. Continue use remotely if extensive work is needed.

Suggested Affirmation:

I love my body and feel the creative force of God flowing through me.
I am perfect the way I am and am very grateful for all things in my life.

Glyph 45 - Male Reproductive System

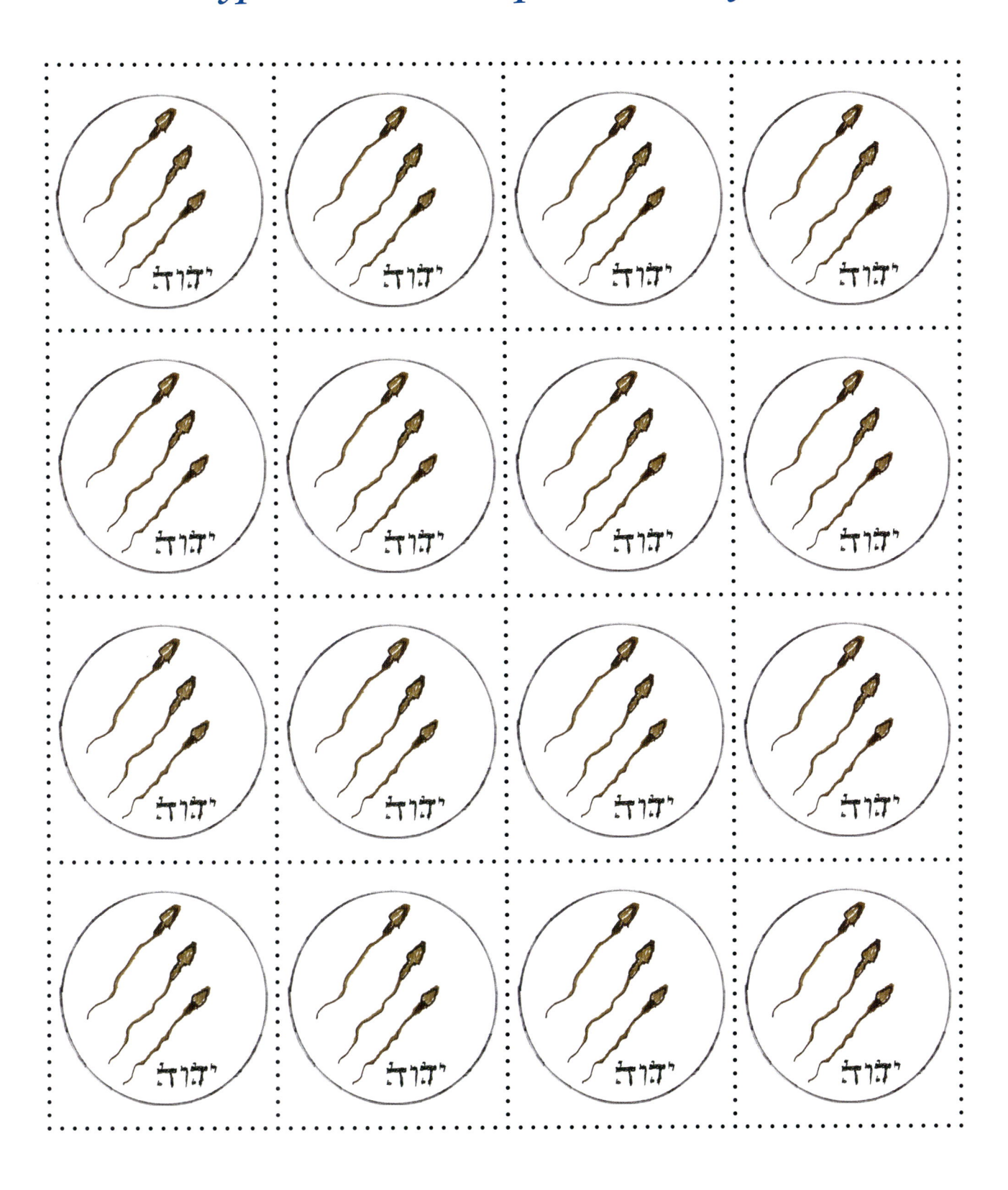

91

Glyph 47 – Thymus Gland

The purpose of this glyph is to clear and regenerate the thymus and remove any associated blockages. The thymus is the gateway to the universe. It also is an important part of your immune system. It usually shrinks as people become older because of excess toxic matter in the body and poor nutrition.

Ways to use this glyph:

Tape the glyph over the thymus at bedtime. Hold a page of these glyphs between the hands as you go to sleep or when you wake up or any other place you feel guided to use it. Also can be used remotely.

Suggested Affirmation:

I see myself as one with God, a pure being of Source energy.
I am one with the Universe and all who reside here.
I am free of any limitations and have only love in my heart for all others.

Glyph 47 – Thymus Gland

Glyph 48 - Thyroid Gland

This glyph is designed to restore a surgically removed thyroid gland or heal a diseased thyroid gland utilizing any needed stem cells and bone marrow plus any other needed frequencies. It can also balance body chemistry and hormone levels as needed during this process plus balance the energies of the right and left hemisphere of the brain bringing the user into real time. It is programmed to incorporate all intrinsic cellular systems to adjust to new frequencies. Understand that under active and over active thyroid are due to emotionally limiting thoughts that must be eliminated and replaced with self love.

Ways to use this glyph:

The glyph should be placed on the throat chakra, solar plexus, heart chakra, held between the hands or put under the feet while sleeping. Also use remotely.

Suggested Affirmation:

I let go of all I hold within me that is not for my highest good and that is not of the Light. It is my intention to always walk in the Light. I love myself and I am perfect the way I am. I see only that which is good in others.

Glyph 48 - Thyroid Gland

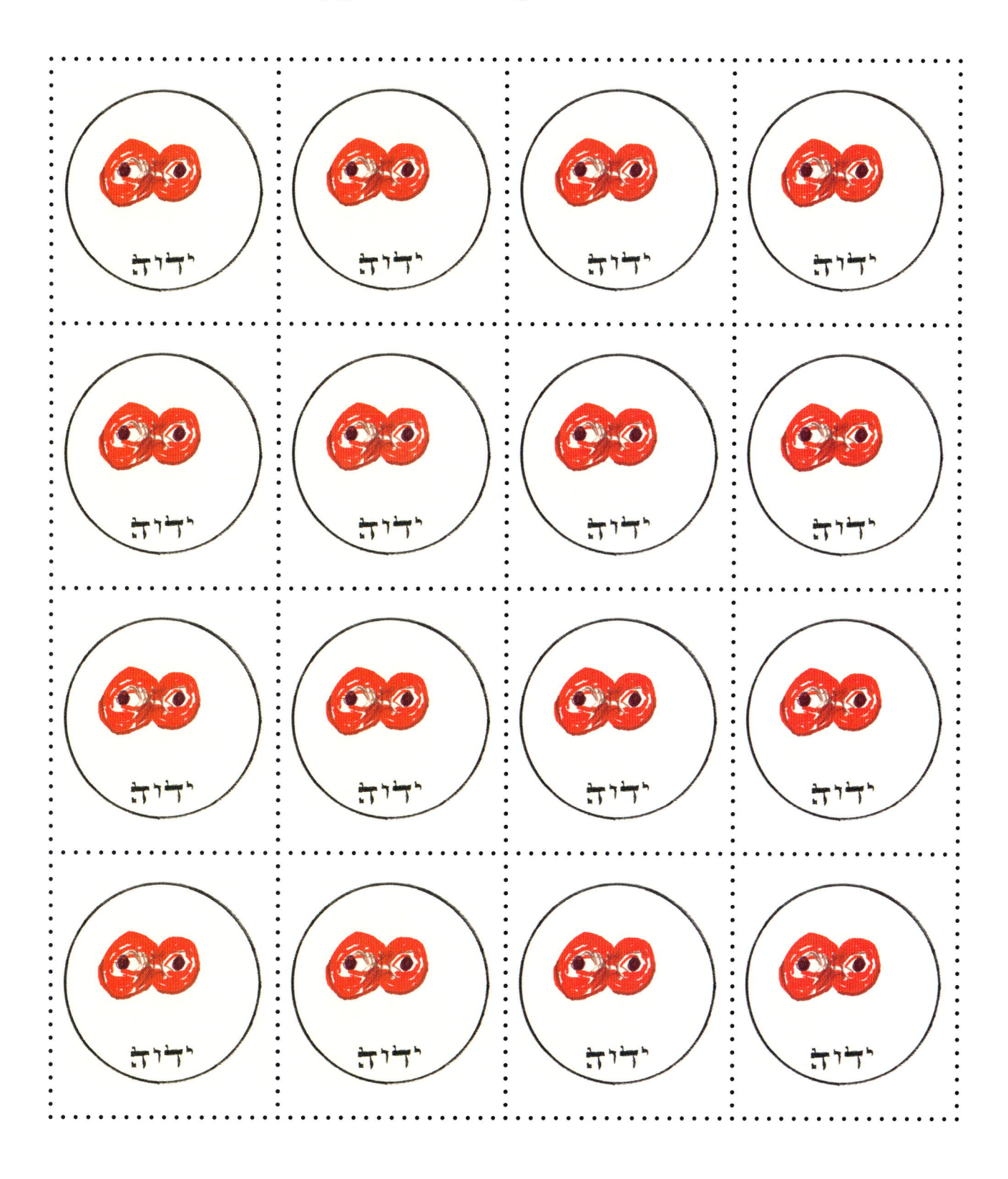

Glyph 57 - Resolve Nerve Damage

This glyph is designed to correct dysfunction of neurons and synovial membrane. It may resolve the tendency to tremors or twitching caused by nerve damage. This glyph stopped twitching in the back leg of my eleven year old dog, Roscoe.

Ways to use this glyph:

Use on the solar plexus and anywhere you feel guided to use it. Hold a block of 6 or 9 glyphs between your hands at bedtime or when waking up. Also try them under your feet at night. Be persistent. I used it a few weeks on my dog before the jerking stopped completely but could only put it on the back of his solar plexus and the chakra above his tail. The more you use them, the faster they work. Remember you must work on releasing the cause. Use the emotional release glyphs in Book I, not just once but every few weeks to release layers of blocked emotions. Also use *Glyph 23* in Book I and *Glyph 96* in this book.

Suggested Affirmation:

I am love in motion. I am clear of any affliction and stand tall without fear or regrets. I am the Light.

Glyph 57 - Resolve Nerve Damage

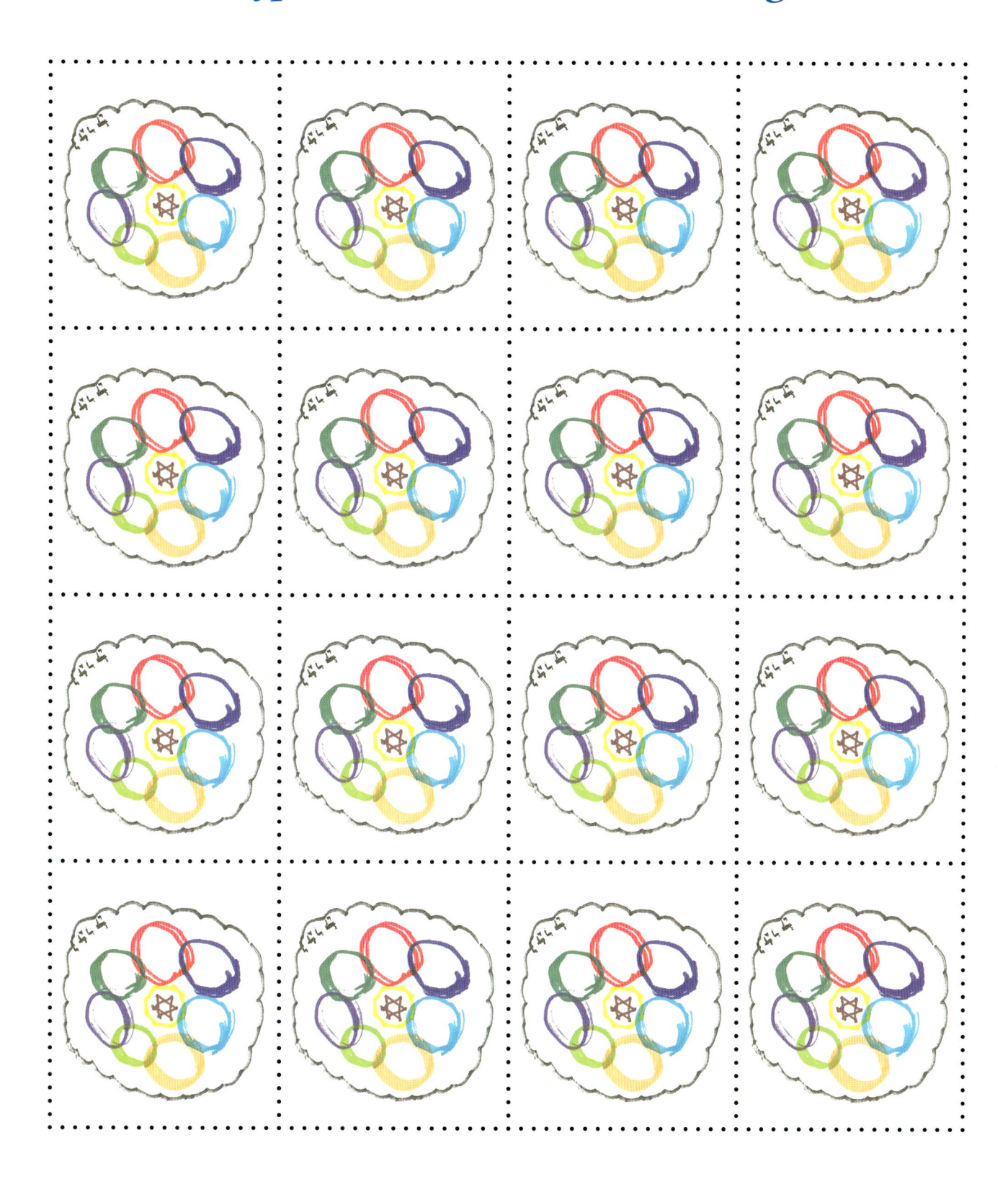

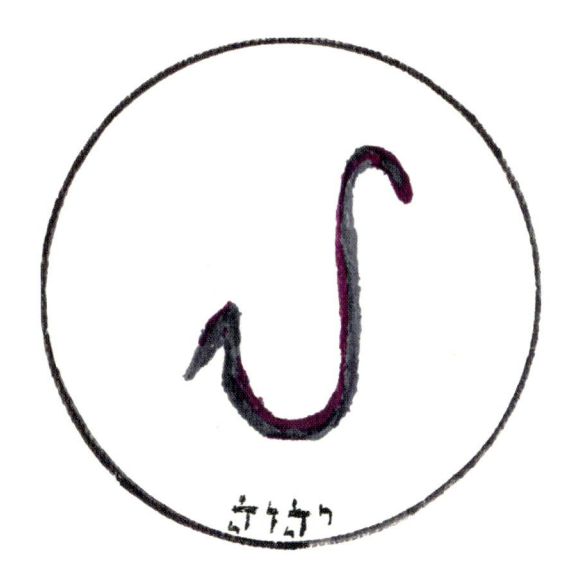

Glyph 60 - Remove Implants

Etheric implants can block one's psychic abilities, interfere with the flow of energy, be used to control, disable or create weird behavior and many other problems. This glyph can extract and transition to Light any etheric implant, device, curse, hex or other negative intentions from the body and the aura that are designed to harm or suppress the individual and that is not there for the highest good. It will also balance the energy of the right and left hemisphere of the brain and establish a self-renewing protective shield around the individual.

Ways to use this glyph:

Cut out a block of 9 or 12 and hold them between your hands while you are going to sleep or when you first wake up. Use on solar plexus.

Suggested Affirmation:

I release any device that has been implanted that is not for my highest good. I am free of any interference and hold myself in the Light. I surround myself with white Light that keeps out any energetic influence that is not for my highest good.

Glyph 60 - Remove Implants

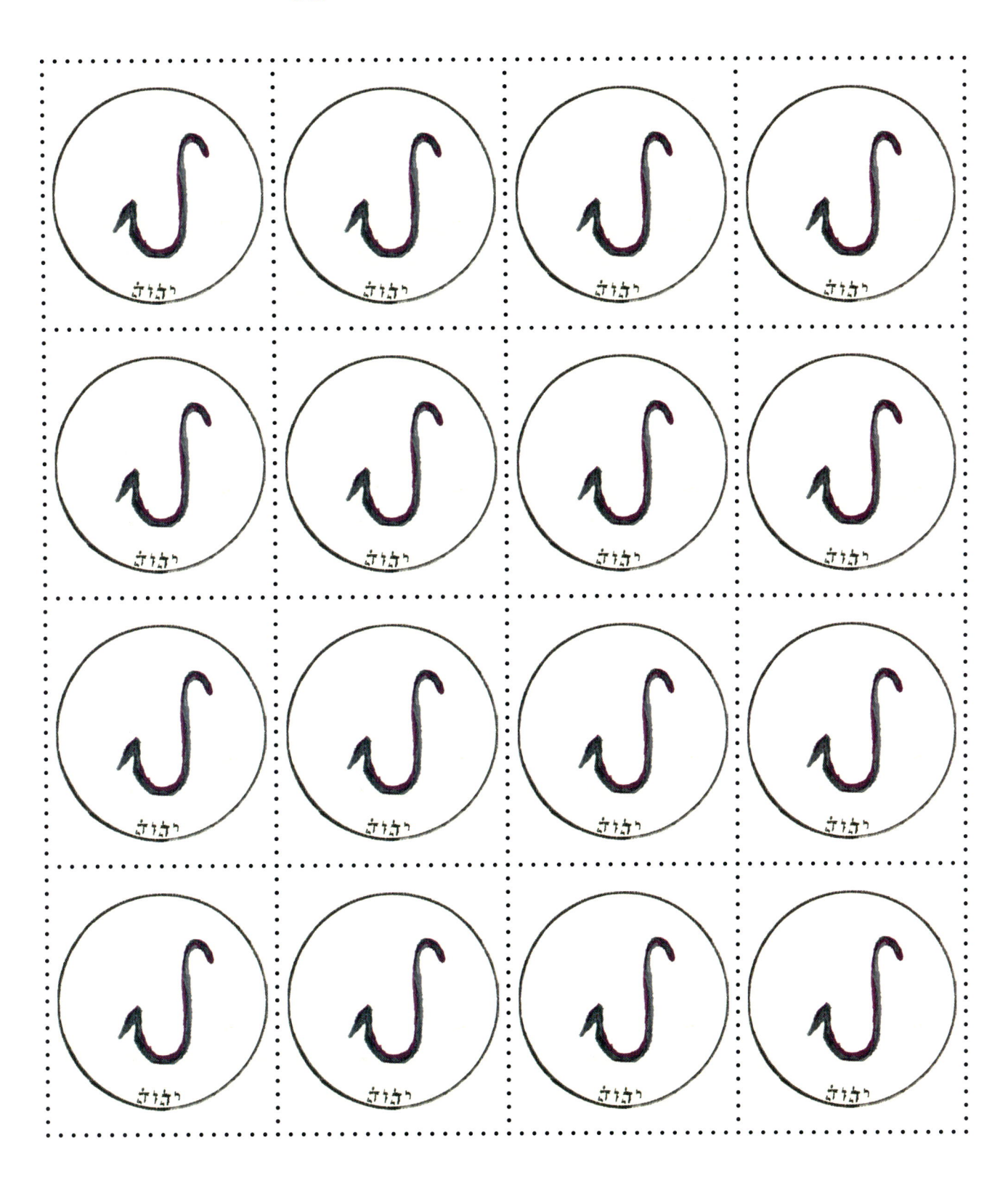

107

Glyph 69 - Malignant Growths

This glyph is programmed to transition malignant cells to Light and heal the damaged area. It can also remove the emotional blockages associated with the malignancy; however, unless the user is willing to understand and change behavior patterns that brought about the cancer, it will often recur. Resentment is the major negative emotion associated with cancer. Resolving a serious malignancy can require changes in diet and other life habits. It also requires use of the detoxification glyphs in both books.

Ways to use this glyph:

Place on any or all major chakras or on affected area. Leave on overnight and use for several days or weeks depending on severity of problem. Also use remotely.

Suggested Affirmation:

I let go of any resentment and see only the Light in others.
I release anything from within me that is not love.
I see myself as a temple of God and know that I am perfect in every way.

Glyph 69 - Malignant Growths

Glyph 70 - Open Consciousness

The purpose of this glyph is to open the individual to their divine right of higher consciousness and access to life purpose agreements. This is a very powerful glyph with 2½ pages of programming to include calling in masters of the angelic realm to work with the person and open access to high vibrational energies and life purpose programs for the individual to remove what is holding them back. Tools can include one or more of the following items such as the BioGenesis Tools, empowered glyphs, color therapies, elixirs, homeopathic remedies, gemstones, herbal remedies, fluids, positive word, integer and number energies, elements, sounds/tones, movement, symbols, sensory and olfactory stimuli, or any other healing element that is deemed appropriate by this team. The intent of this work is to raise the light radiant factor of the Earth incarnated soul, the physical and energy selves of this soul up to and including the Goddess/God energies and to assist the incarnated soul in obtaining its highest potential and goals for this lifetime. This work may spread out over several days.

Ways to use this glyph:

You may wear this glyph on the solar plexus at night but also use this glyph remotely for a few days. Spend time in meditation. To use this on others, please ask their permission first or ask permission from their soul. It may take many sessions to remove serious negativity. In all cases, the persons' free will prevails.

> ### *Suggested Affirmation:*
> I ask for divine assistance in releasing all that is holding me back from understanding who I am and why I am here. I remove from myself anything that is not love. I ask for the codes and keys to my awakening.

Glyph 70 - Open Consciousness

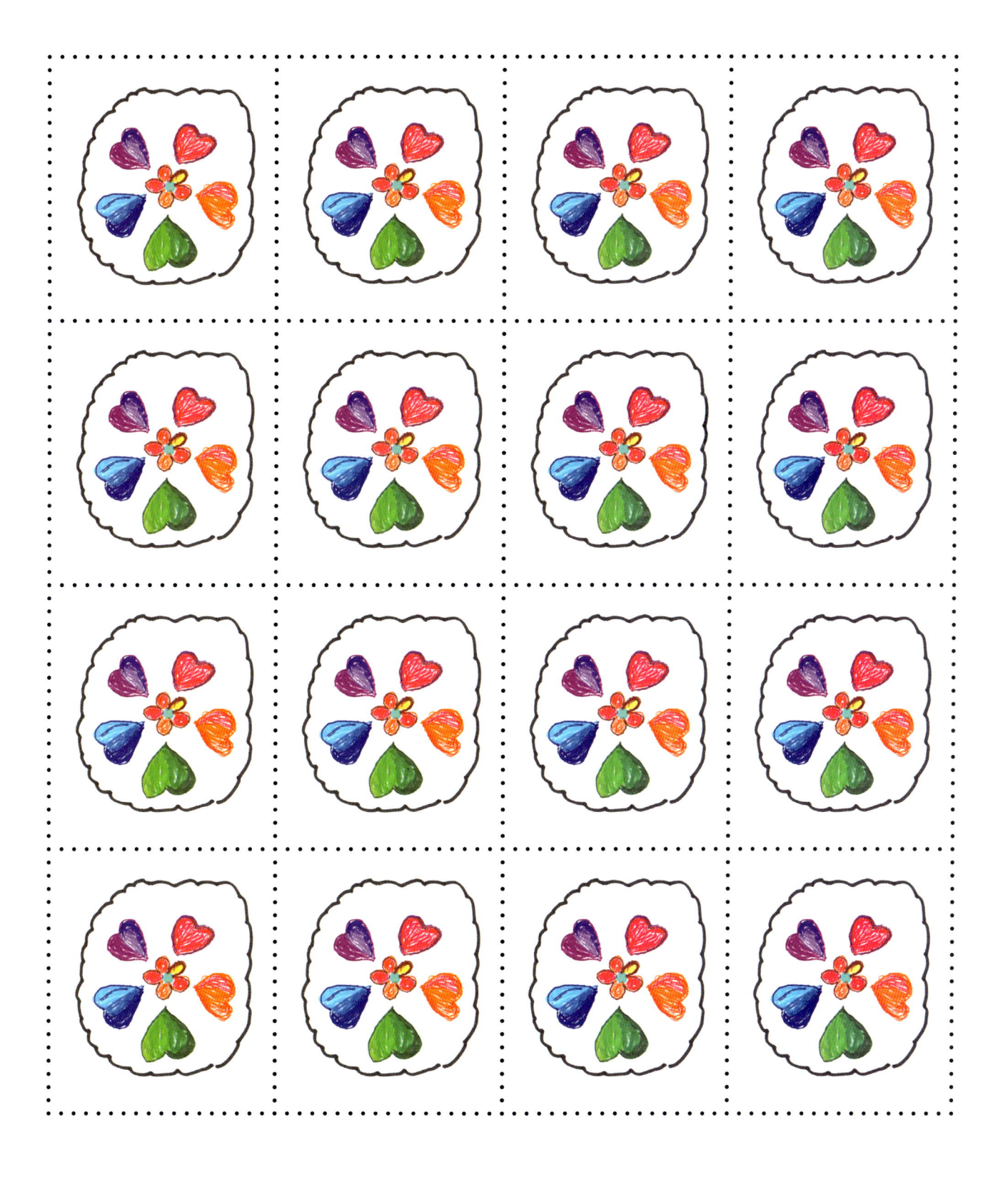

Glyph 72 - Marijuana

The purpose of this glyph is to send the frequency of marijuana into the body to be used as a healing tool when it is for the highest good of the user. Medical marijuana can be very helpful in providing comfort and healing to persons experiencing various illnesses. Good results have been reported from persons with Irritable Bowel Syndrome. Do not use this glyph while driving a motor vehicle.

Ways to use this glyph:

For nervous bowel problems place a block of the glyphs over the abdomen to include the navel. Also use on the solar plexus. Use any way you feel guided to use this.

Suggested Affirmation:
I see myself as well, whole and perfect in all ways.
I am filled with joy as I know that I am healed.

Glyph 72 - Marijuana

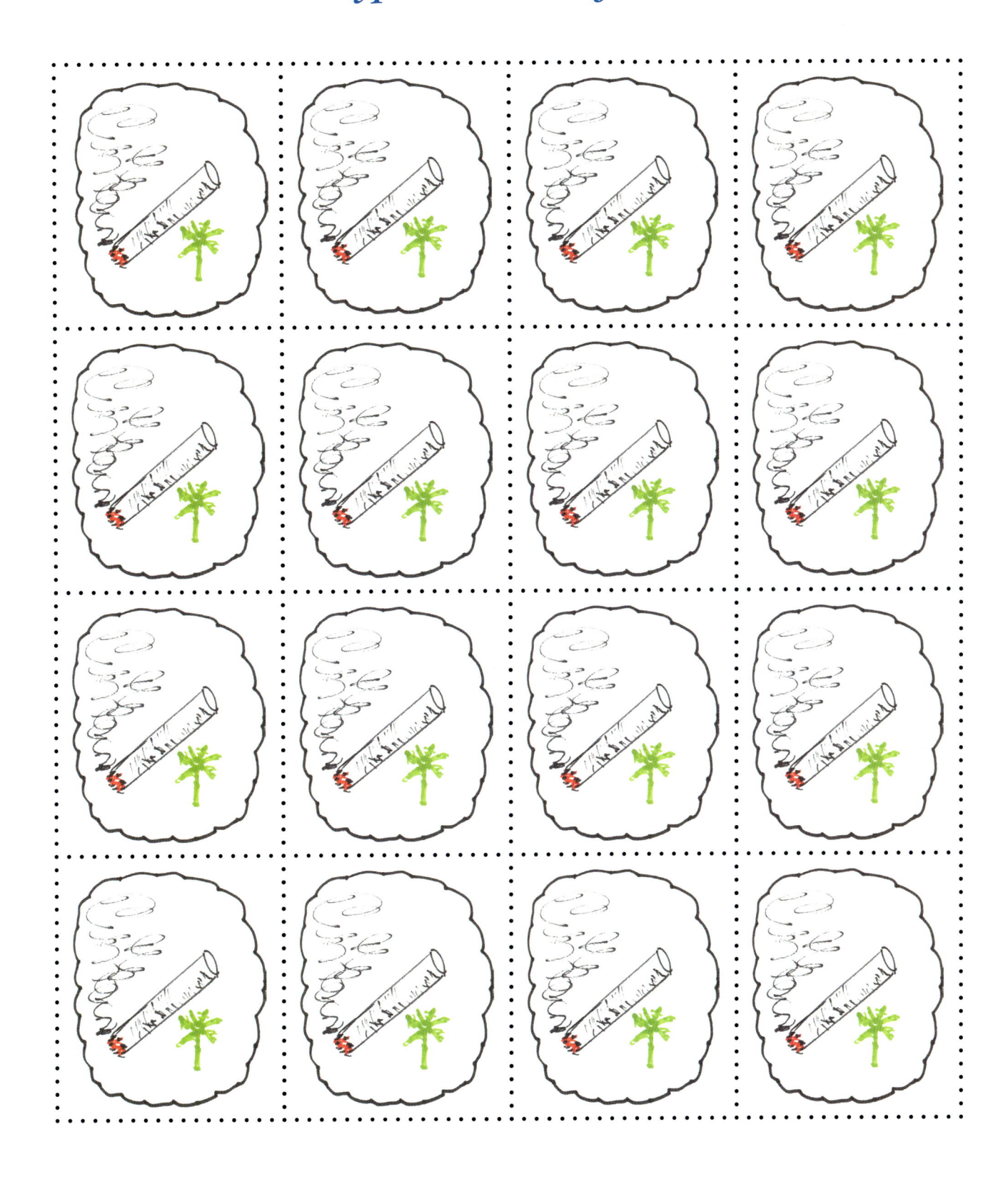

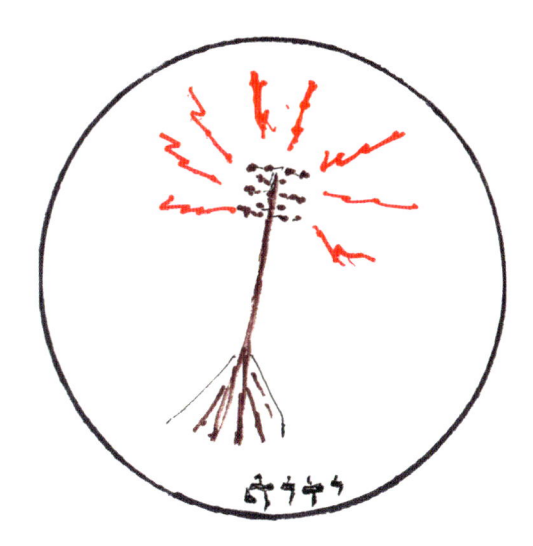

Glyph 86 - Electromagnetic Frequencies

This glyph can protect the user from any electromagnetic frequencies such as cell phone towers, microwaves, televisions, etc. It can also be placed on cordless phones, cell phones, hair dryers or any other electrical devices to prevent their emissions from affecting the user.

Ways to use this glyph:

Tape to cordless phones, cell phone or any other electrical devices or outlets and fuse boxes. Place this glyph on the solar plexus to protect from electrical emissions.

Suggested Affirmation:
I surround myself with White Light that is impenetrable by any energy that is not in harmony with my body.

Glyph 86 - Electromagnetic Frequencies

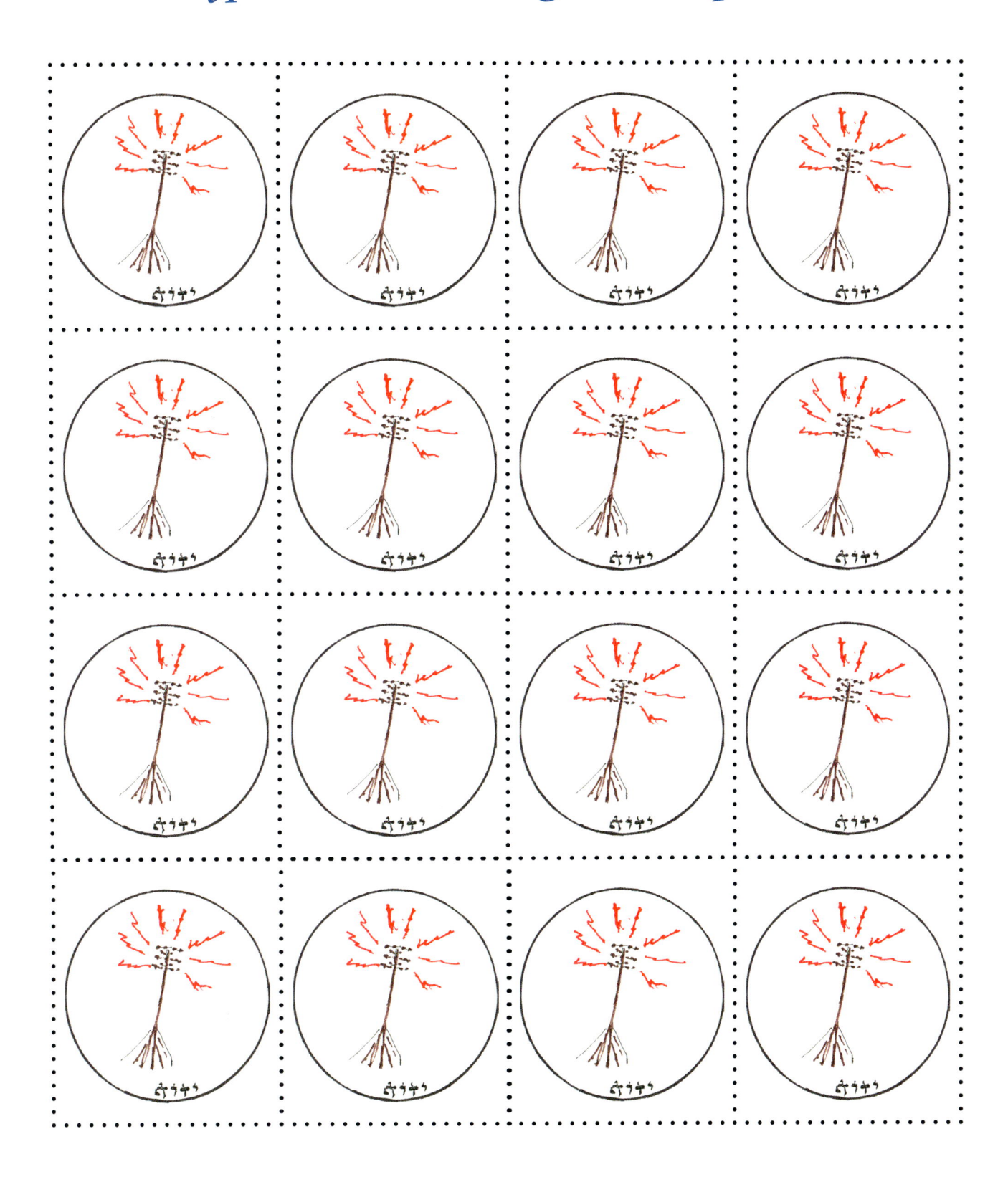

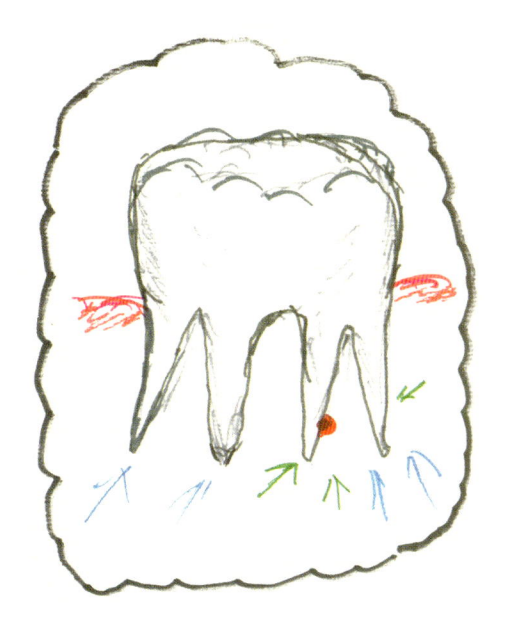

Glyph 88 - Abscessed Tooth

This glyph can resolve the infection in the abscessed tooth. It is also programmed to restore the root; however, the success of root restoration will depend on the actual source of the infection, which is most often in another location of the body. For example, if the source of the infection is a congested colon or another organ filled with toxins and parasites, the root of the tooth cannot heal until the source of the problem is resolved.

Ways to use this glyph:

Use on solar plexus, any major chakra or where you feel guided to use it. This glyph should also be used remotely after the infection has subsided.

Suggested Affirmation:
All areas of my body that need healing are experiencing it right now.
I am filled with the Light and love of my Creator.

Glyph 88 - Abscessed Tooth

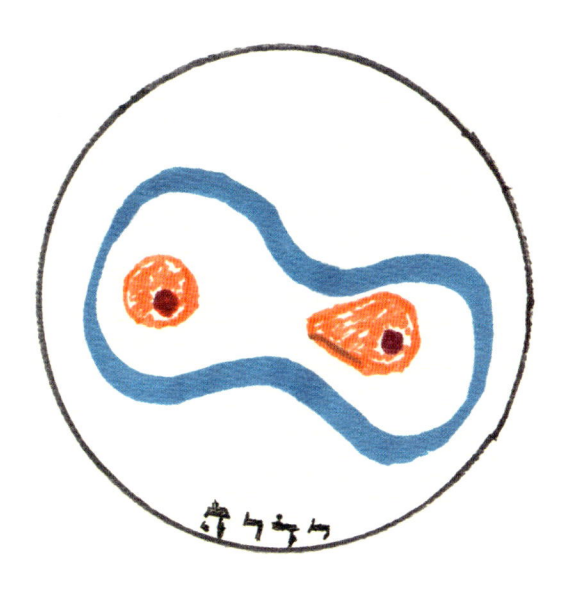

Glyph 89 - Restore Surgically Removed Tonsils

This glyph is empowered to restore surgically removed tonsils utilizing any needed stem cells and bone marrow plus any other needed frequencies. It can restore the function of the tonsils as they are being regenerated. It can also balance body chemistry and hormone levels as needed during this process plus balance the energies of the right and left hemisphere of the brain bringing the user into real time, and incorporate all intrinsic cellular systems to adjust to new frequencies. See page 11 on restoring surgically removed body parts.

Ways to use this glyph:

The glyph should be placed on the solar plexus, heart chakra, held between the hands or put under the feet while sleeping. After a couple of days place a sheet of these glyphs in a secure place, a bookcase or table with a sheet of paper instructing the glyph to continue sending the direction and energy to all major chakras of your body (using your name). Place your intent and belief in the ability of this to work.

Suggested Affirmation:

I let go of all I hold within me that is not for my highest good and that is not of the Light. I am grateful for the many blessings that have come to me. Thank you God for all that I receive.

Glyph 89 - Restore Surgically Removed Tonsils

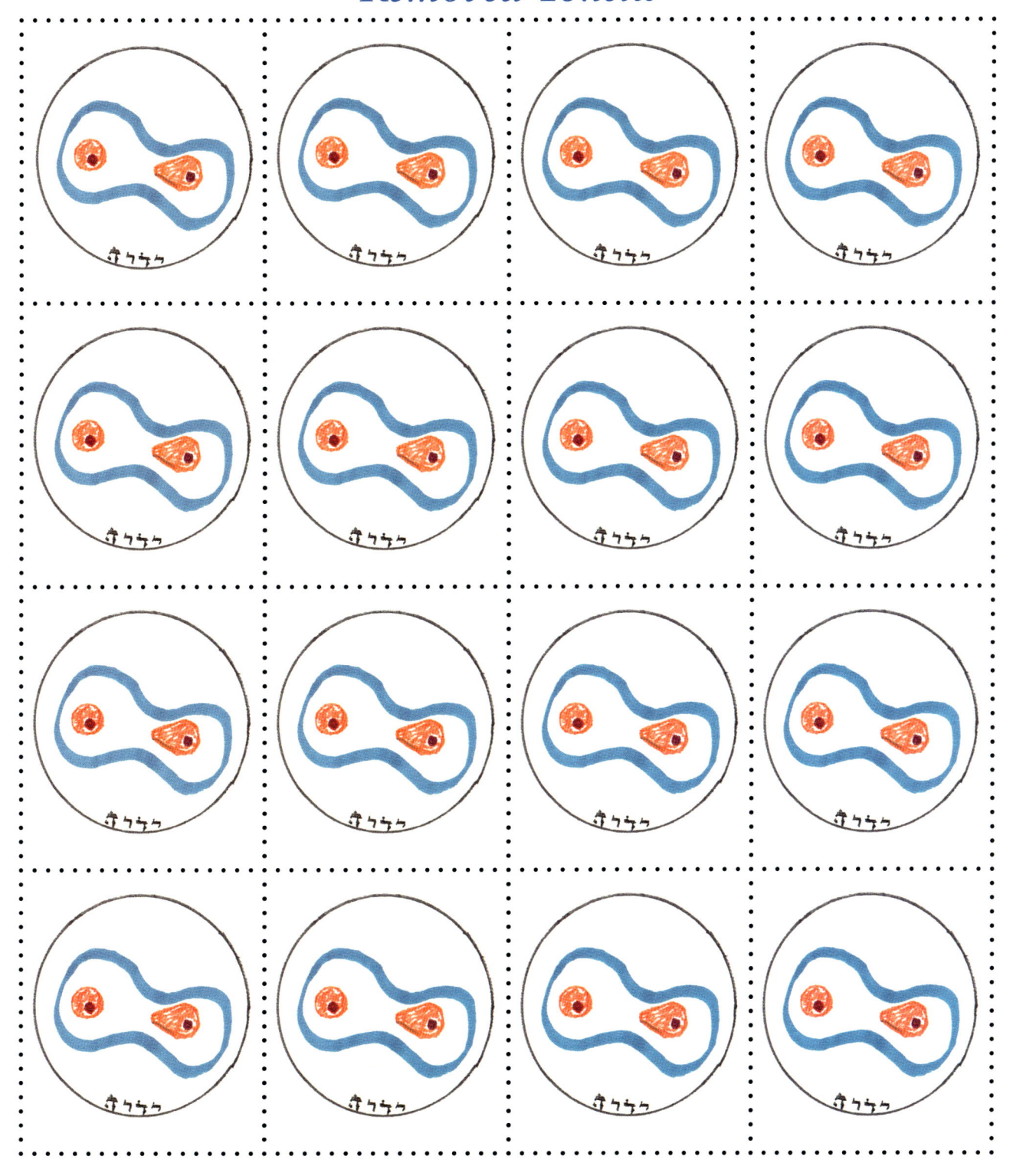

131

Glyph 93 - Candida and Intestinal Support

This glyph can transition an overgrowth of yeast or fungus within the body and heal and rebuild the intestinal tract. It can transition die-off as well and purify the blood.

Ways to use this glyph:

Cover the abdomen with a page of these glyphs. Put them inside a bootie to wear under your feet at night. Yeast cells can also invade the brain. Take a page of glyphs and hold between the hands when going to sleep or waking up. Use any other way you feel guided to use them. You will also need to follow an alkaline diet to prevent reoccurrence. Use the emotional healing glyphs from Book I to resolve the cause.

Suggested Affirmation:

Recognizing the power within me as an extension of Source Energy, I release all I hold that is preventing me from digesting and assimilating what I need for my sustenance. I move forward with my life with joy and ease. I believe in my power. Thank you Creator for all the blessings and assistance that I receive.

Glyph 93 - Candida and Intestinal Support

Glyph 94 - Allergies

This glyph is designed to detect allergies in the body, pinpoint whether they are physical, emotional or genetic and resolve the disturbance they cause, stopping allergic response in the body and promote healing. It will also purify the blood and strengthen the immune system, resolve swelling and congestion and end systemic allergic reactions when used over a period of time. It will also balance the energies of the right and left hemisphere of the brain. It will be important to work on resolving denial of your own power.

Ways to use this glyph:

This glyph should be placed on the solar plexus, heart chakra or any major chakra. Continued use can gradually resolve reoccurrence of symptoms. Continue to use this glyph remotely for best results.

Suggested Affirmation:

I let go of all I hold within me that is not for my highest good and that is not of the Light. I am grateful for the many blessings that have come to me. I affirm that I am a powerful being of Light that has no limitations.

Glyph 94 - Allergies

Glyph 95 - Lymphatic Cleansing

This glyph can resolve problems with congested lymph when used consistently.

Ways to use this glyph:

Put page of glyphs on pads to wear under the feet while sleeping. If feeling is too intense, try again until the glyph can be tolerated. Place on any or all major chakras or on affected area. Place page of glyphs between the hands while lying on your side or over solar plexus with both hands on glyphs when lying on your back. Length of time needed will depend on severity of condition.

Suggested Affirmation:
I am free and healthy. Nothing is disturbing the joy that fills me.
I see myself as a fountain of love.

Glyph 95 - Lymphatic Cleansing

Glyph 96 - Resolving Neurological Problems

This glyph can resolve many different types of neurological problems. It can transition matter that encumbers the nervous system and repair damaged or missing chromosome markers. It can also balance the endocrine system and resolve any chemical imbalance.

Ways to use this glyph:

Tape this glyph to the solar plexus while sleeping or put on any major chakra you feel guided to use. Wear under feet at night. Severe problems can require a longer period of use.

Suggested Affirmation:

I send peace and healing energy to my entire nervous system.
I am calm, well and bless my body.
Thank you God for helping me with this healing.

Glyph 96 - Resolving Neurological Problems

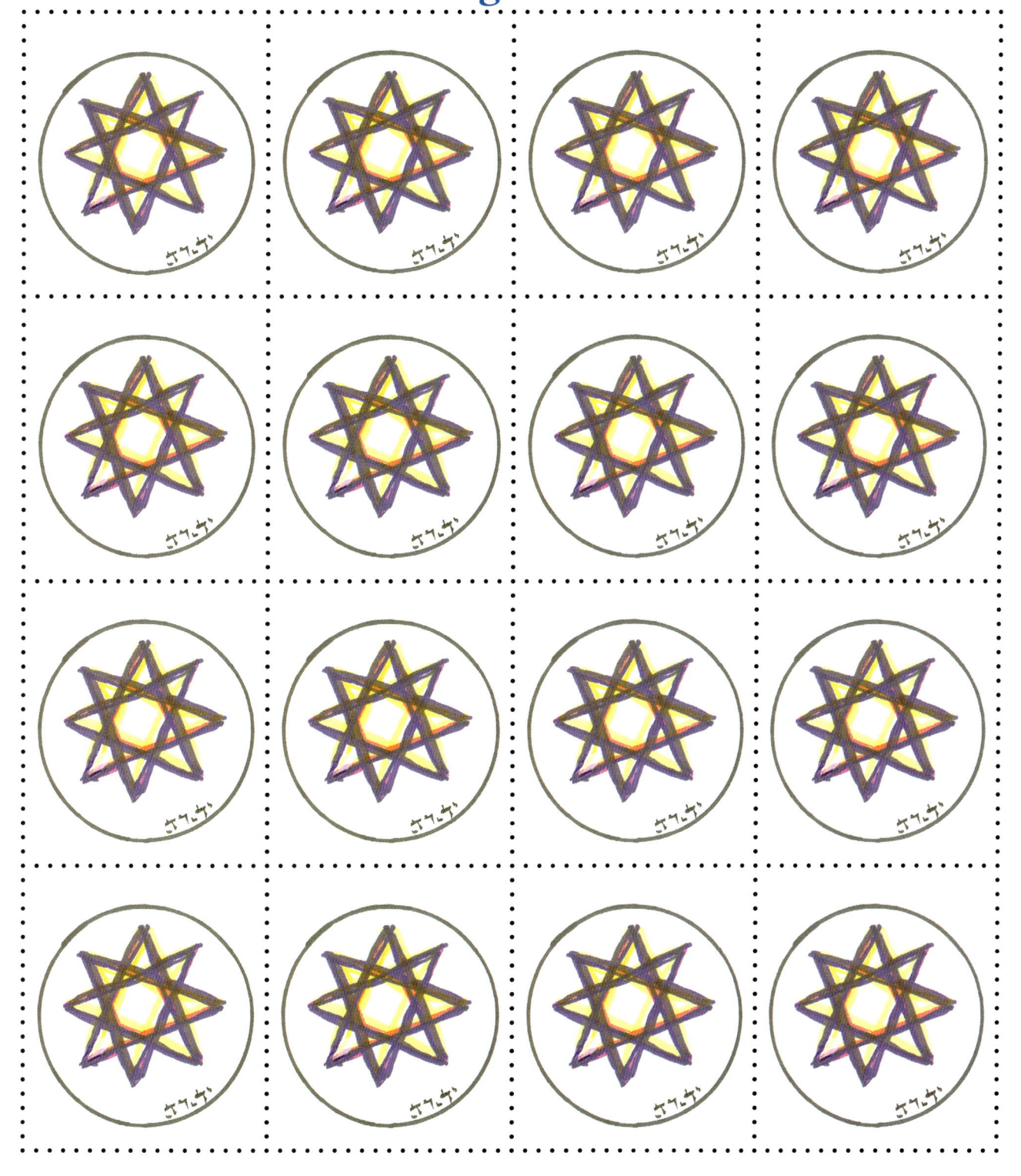

Glyph 97 - Checkerboard

This glyph can help remove blockages and imprint directives that enhance the ability to communicate with all influences that are in service to the Light and the Divine Plan. It can also remove implants that prevent course correction or impede progress as well as remove anything that will prevent Light Sources from instilling Divine direction. This is conditional on the will of the user. The user must be ready and willing to release attraction to outside influences of dark directives.

Ways to use this glyph:

Place on the solar plexus or hold block of 9 or 12 between the hands when going to sleep or first waking up in the morning. The Affirmation is very critical for requesting the codes and keys for Divine awakening.

Suggested Affirmation:
It is my desire to be of service to the Divine in whatever way I am needed. I ask for the codes and keys to bring about my awakening and to be guided to my highest Light and my greatest growth.

Glyph 97 - Checkerboard

Glyph 99 - Energy

This glyph can energize and rejuvenate the lower Dan Tian (below the navel) and Snow Mountain areas (lower back). This can help to energize the body and enhance the immune system. It can also enhance the ability to hear messages from spirit.

Ways to use this glyph:

Place on the solar plexus, heart chakra or sacral chakra. Use any other way you feel guided to use this glyph.

Suggested Affirmation:

As I feel the breath of the Divine energy flowing through me, I express my gratitude. I accept myself as a part of Source energy and hold myself in the Light.

Glyph 99 - Energy

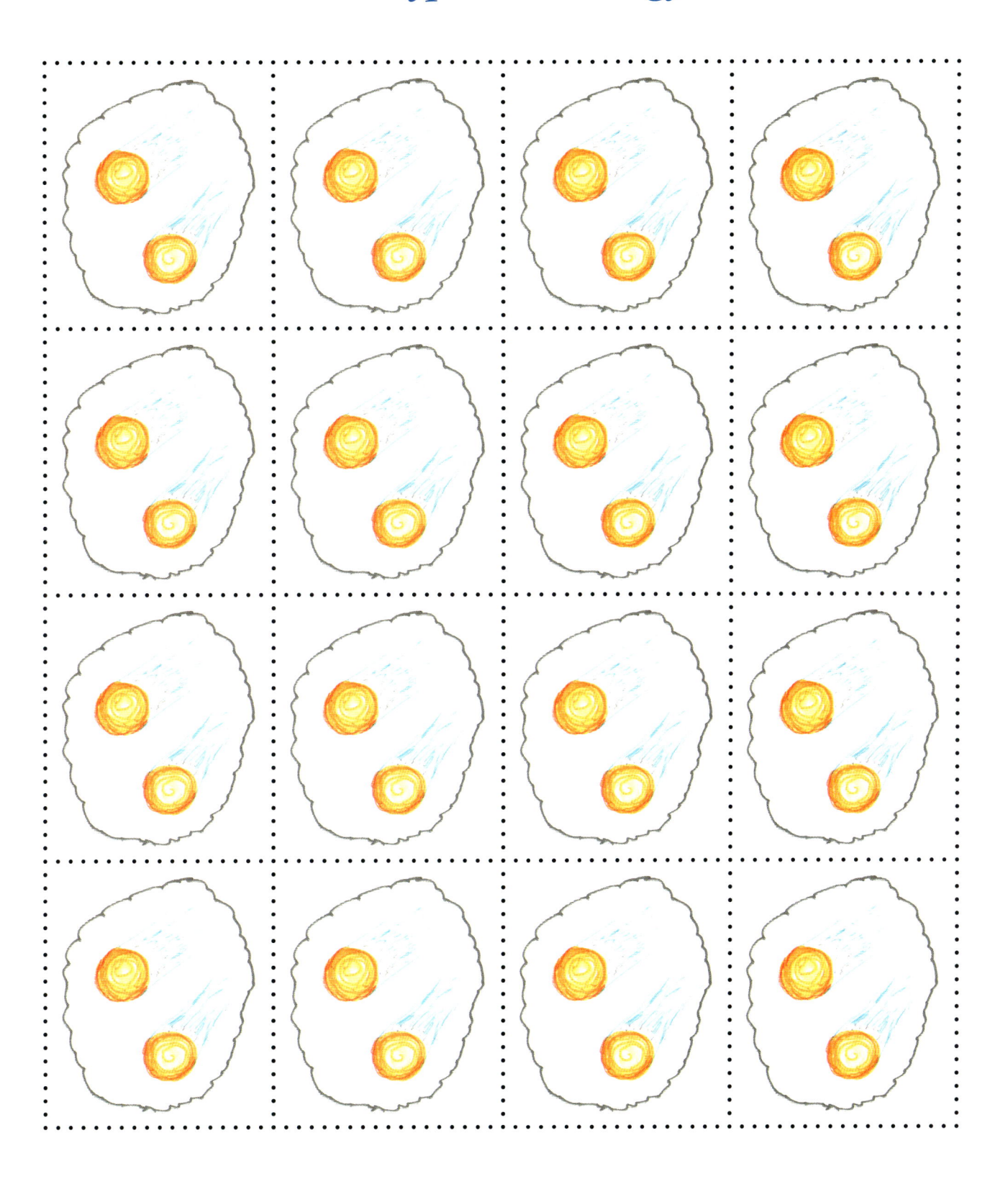

Appendix A

Locating the Chakras

These drawings are provided to help you locate the chakras. If you put your hand on top of your head you will feel a warm spot. (This may be more difficult to locate if you are bald.) There is a slightly warm spot at the location of each of the other chakras that is easier to notice through a bulky material. If you are still unsure that you have the right location, cut a group of four of the glyphs to insure coverage of the right chakra.

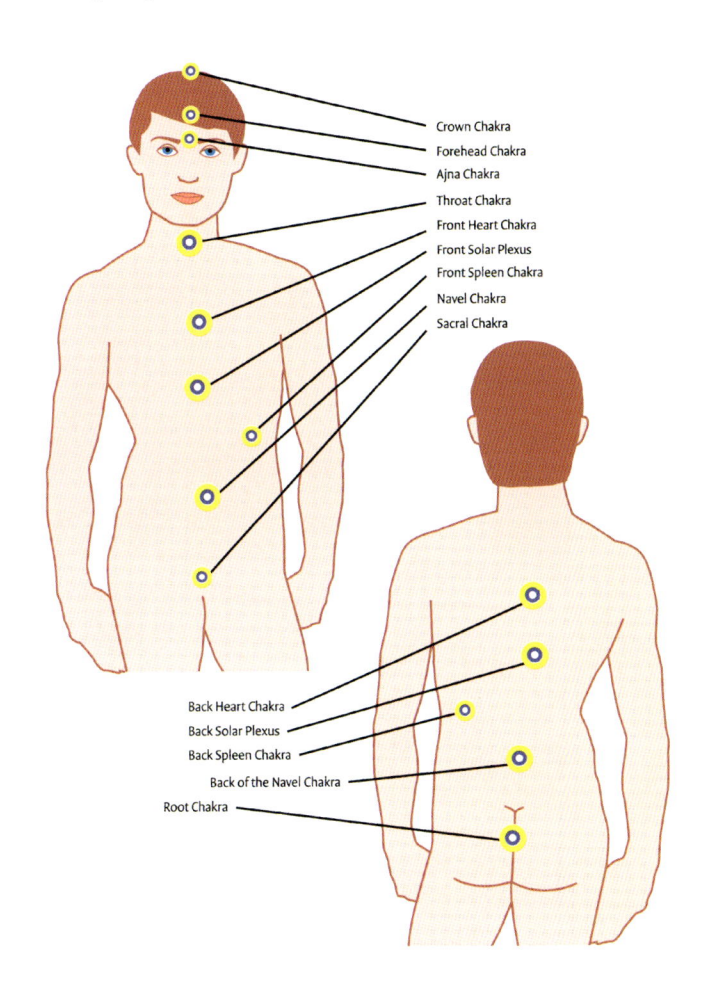

Crown Chakra
Forehead Chakra
Ajna Chakra
Throat Chakra
Front Heart Chakra
Front Solar Plexus
Front Spleen Chakra
Navel Chakra
Sacral Chakra

Back Heart Chakra
Back Solar Plexus
Back Spleen Chakra
Back of the Navel Chakra
Root Chakra

Major Chakra Points on a Human

The chakras of an animal can also be located by a warm spot through their hair or fur. It is easier to locate and position a glyph on the back side of the animal. This should be done when they are sleeping. Dowsing Charts are provided in Appendix C to help you locate what glyphs you need and where to put them. Instructions are also provided. This drawing of a dog is provided to show the location of the backside chakras. The front or underside will be directly opposite. The chakras on a cat are in the same location as they are on a dog. Concentrate on the pet or a picture of the pet when dowsing.

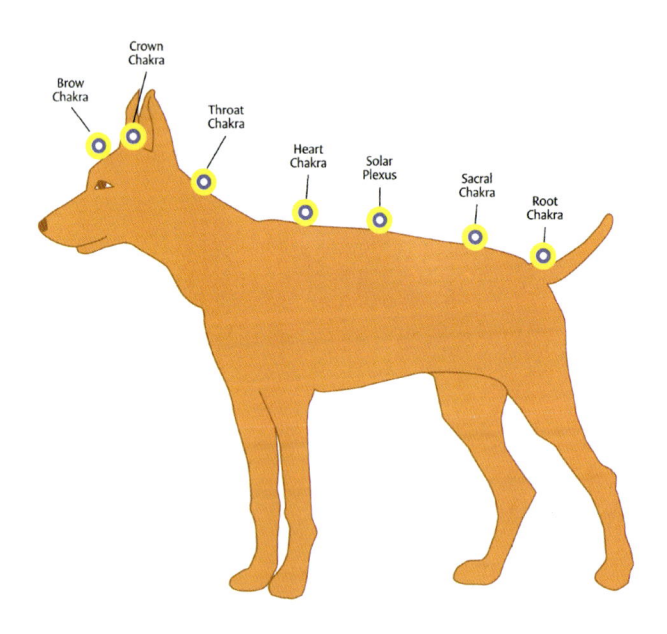

Major Chakra Points on a Dog (or Cat)

Appendix B

AcuTapping

AcuTapping, also known as *Thought Field Therapy or Emotional Release Technique*, is another powerful way to remove negative emotions when they are in our present thoughts. By tapping with our fingers on various acupuncture points, we can release these negative emotions easily and quickly. Memorize the Basic Tapping Sequence below. Use this on any emotional or physical problem by customizing it with an appropriate Setup Statement and Reminder Phrase. Be persistent until all parts of the problem have vanished. Try it on anything and everything! It either works or it does no harm.

Basic Technique

Make a note (mental or written) of what specific problem is bothering you at this time. Rate how much it is affecting you on a scale from 0 to 10, with zero being no effect and ten the greatest effect imaginable.

1. The Setup: Make the following statement or a similar statement while continuously tapping (or massaging) the collarbone area with two or three fingers (you can use one or two hands): "Even though I have this [state specific problem], I deeply and completely accept myself the way I am."

2. The Sequence: (Repeat 3 times) With two or three fingers or the whole hand, tap five times (or massage an equal amount of time) on each of the following energy points while repeating a one or two word Reminder Phrase to keep you focused on your specific problem. Under the eyes, collar bone and four inches under the arm pit on your left side. Repeat this three times and then recheck your 0 to 10 level. The ideal goal is to repeat until you are at zero. See Figure 1.

3. The sequence is terminated. Rate again how much the original problem is affecting you on the scale from 0 to 10. If there is still a problem, repeat Step 1 and 2 until you reach a zero.

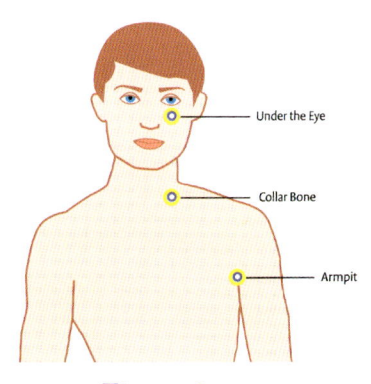

Figure 1

Appendix C - Dowsing

An excellent method of finding out which glyph you need (or your pet needs) is through dowsing. This manual will state briefly how dowsing works, but for a thorough explanation, it is strongly recommended that you purchase the book, *Letter to Robin: A Mini Course in Pendulum Dowsing* by Walt Woods. The charts on the next page are designed to help you locate which glyphs are needed and where they should be placed on the body. Dowsing of this type is done with a pendulum, which can be purchased at any gem and crystal shop. A pendulum is a very useful tool that can provide you with answers to many questions. Once you have your pendulum, program it by telling it which direction you want it to swing for a yes answer (usually back and forth in front of you) and what way it should swing for a no (side to side). Remember, you tell the pendulum, it does not tell you. It is important to clear your mind of any outcome or your own energy will cause the pendulum to swing in the direction your mind is telling it, rather than the universal energy that would give you the correct answer. A little practice will help you considerably. It does not matter if you make a mistake and select a glyph that is not needed, or put it on the wrong place. The worst that can happen is nothing. No harm can come from any of the glyphs. They are completely safe.

When selecting a pendulum, pick one that feels right to you. It does not matter what it is made of but should have sufficient weight to have a good swing. Use the charts often since your needs will change as you continue to release more and more. The prayer glyphs are an easy, pain free method of healing. They are completely safe.

There are three charts for the glyph numbers. The fourth chart is for the location on your body that you should place the glyph. After you have used your pendulum to locate the glyph that will help you, go right to the fourth chart to find out where you should place the glyph without looking to see the name or number. This will help prevent you from trying to guess where the glyph should go. You may be surprised at where the pendulum tells you to put the glyph. Remember, everything is connected.

Glyph Dowsing Chart #1 (11-40)

11 12 20 21 28 31 32 33 34 35 36 37 38 39

Glyph Dowsing Chart #1
"Which Glyph Will Help Me?"

162

Glyph Dowsing Chart #2 (41-93)

Glyph Dowsing Chart #2
"Which Glyph Will Help Me?"

41, 43, 44, 45, 47, 48, 57, 60, 69, 70, 72, 86, 88, 89, 93

Glyph Dowsing Chart #3 (94-99)

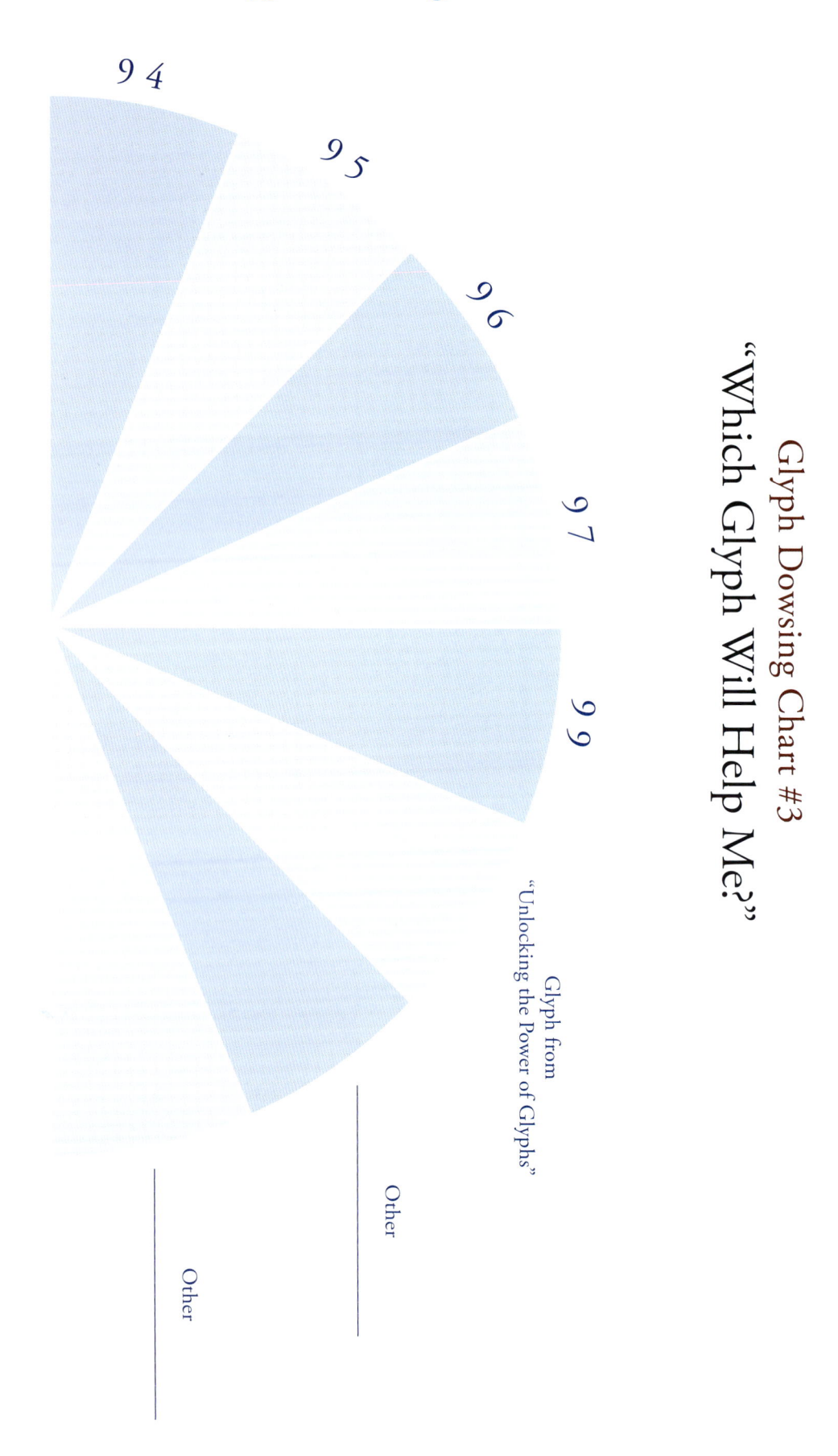

"Which Glyph Will Help Me?"
Glyph Dowsing Chart #3

94
95
96
97
99

Glyph from "Unlocking the Power of Glyphs"

Other

Other

Glyph Dowsing Chart #4

"Where do I need to apply glyph #____?"

- solar plexus posterior
- heart posterior
- throat posterior
- back of head
- naval
- back of naval
- spleen
- liver
- bottom of feet
- hands
- other
- root
- sacral
- solar plexus
- heart
- throat
- third eye
- crown
- sacral posterior

Appendix D

A Few of Many Testimonials

Glyph heals dog:

On Saturday night our little Yorkeepoo, Belle, was sitting on the floor acting very strange. I picked her up and she was drooling excessively, her nose was warm, her eyes were glazed and she was disoriented. Since it was Saturday night we could not take her to the vet. We had just purchased Jean Logan's book of glyphs a few days earlier and saw it sitting right near by so I (Beverly) cut out three of the Anti-Bacterial/Virus glyphs and following the drawing in the book, put one on her crown chakra, one on the back of her neck and one on the back of her solar plexus. We said the prayer together and affirmed our belief that she would be well. We could hardly hear her breathe and her heart beat felt very faint. I lay down in bed holding her. About 1:30 in the morning she jumped up acting very perky, her nose was cold and her eyes were clear and bright again. The next day she was completely normal. We are so grateful.

Beverly Allen and Raymond Braziel
Franklin, NC

Glyph restores man's virility:

I have just recently been introduced to Jean Logan's book, "Unlocking the Power of Glyphs". Having never heard of this modality of healing before, I quickly scanned through the book checking out all the different purposes for which the glyphs can be used. One in particular really "jumped out" at me, which was titled Repair Damaged Nerves. I had felt for years that I had nerve damage due to past substance abuse, namely crystal methamphetamine and cocaine, the aftermath of which left me severely unable to focus. I worried about almost everything and generally had trouble just keeping on top of my game in life.

I put the glyph above my eyebrows, which is the third eye chakra, read the affirmation for this glyph and laid back for about 15 minutes. I could feel lots of intense energy as if a loving hand was holding the glyph down. After about 15 minutes I got up. I immediately was aware that I had energy but it was a calm, focused energy which I rarely had felt before trying the glyph. I found that I was alert but calm. This feeling maintained until I went to bed. I slept very well that night and was completely relaxed. The next morning I woke up feeling really good and well rested. I got up and looked at the clock thinking I had overslept. It was an hour earlier than I normally get up. I felt so good I stayed up! Then something happened that was totally unexpected. I got fiercely sexually aroused. I had not felt this way since pre-meth days and had pretty much resigned myself to the fact that I had killed my sex drive by using meth. It was back all the way. I felt like a 20-year-old again. When I did finally have an orgasm, I felt it through every fiber of my being!

I have done what I consider to be a lot of spiritual and energy work. I consider the result I got from this first glyph that I used to be one of the most dramatic and powerful results of any modality thus tried. The glyphs do exactly what it says they do. I have used other glyphs and have had equally powerful if not more powerful results.

To Jean, thank you for bringing this to our world when we need it most. You are truly an instrument of Thy peace.

Love, Dave

Infection stopped:

After giving myself a pedicure, I found myself with an infection behind the nail of the large toe on my left foot. The toe was red, swollen and very painful. I wrapped the Anti Bacterial glyph around it and taped it in place before going to bed. The next morning the pain, swelling and redness was completely gone. Two weeks later the skin was peeling off where the infection had been.

Jeanne

Glyphs help dog's anxiety:

I know that the energy that creates worlds can also be used for healing with the animal kingdom which is so lovingly part of our universal energy. I have used glyphs on myself and have had amazing, powerful results, so I decided to try them on my parents' dog, Ginger, who is a rather large mixed breed, but a real wuss during a thunderstorm. She would normally not leave my side during a storm and would tremble even while petting. I used the glyph for fear, taping it to her forehead. Not only did she stop shaking, she went happily around the house, and I actually had forgotten about her until later I noticed the glyph still taped to her forehead! I used another glyph on Ginger when my parents went away for a long weekend. Ginger was beside herself with anguish and was whining profusely. I used the glyph for abandonment just to see if it would quiet her down. She was quiet for the rest of the night, and when I went upstairs where her sleeping area was, she was still sleeping with it next to her. It is so rewarding to see the miracle of healing working so consistently in the animal kingdom and to see the relief of pain that is possible with a little faith and a glyph.

David

Injured wrist helped by glyph:

Several months ago I broke my left wrist. Since I was in Peru when it happened, it was not set correctly. I have been back in Atlanta undergoing physical therapy for the wrist for several months. The therapy has not been going well. My doctor advised me that about 30% percent recovery was the most I could expect. So I contacted my friend, Jean Logan, author of the powerful book, "Unlocking the Power of Glyphs." She provided me with the glyph on bones, cartilage and ligaments. The first day my fingers tingled for the first time since the injury when I placed the glyph under my wrist as the author had instructed me. The next day both the fingers and wrist not only tingled, but I could feel energy coming from the wrist. As of today, just a week after I began using the glyphs, I have much more flexibility in both the wrist and fingers of the damaged hand. I estimate that in just one week my recovery has gone from 30% to 50%. I feel confident that the damaged hand will continue to get better. The most spiritual person I know, Jean Logan is a modern day healer. I highly recommend "Unlocking the Power of Glyphs."

Leon Jones

A phenomenal book, endowed with gently powerful healing energy! Touch any glyph--you can feel it all over. I strongly recommend it. Unexpectedly, it comes with several copies of each, for clipping and pasting or carrying with you, usable in a multitude of situations. I've tried it--it works!

Ellen Bauer

As a Spiritual Healing practitioner I use many healing tools in my practice. The book "Unlocking the Power of the Glyphs" is a valued addition to my collection. These tools have increased the healing potential for each client without increasing the amount of time invested in a healing session. This provides an overall increase in the level of satisfaction that I provide to my clients without increasing the session cost. A win-win situation for all!

I would highly recommend this book as an addition to any practitioners tool kit or to anyone who wants to experience accelerated healing. The text is easy to read and the Appendixes provide additional reference material and charts. No experience necessary to use the tools!

Thanks to Jean Logan for bringing this wealth of information to humanity. I am looking forward to the second book!

Debbie Winter

When I dowse to see what glyph to use - which is the only way I choose glyphs - and I am told to wear the abundance glyph, marvelous events occur. New clients, new opportunities, and my husband got a raise and his company said that they weren't giving out raises this year again (it has been 3 years since anyone has received a raise.) We live totally in the mindset of abundance so that to my mind isn't an issue for us, but it has really been fun to have these new channels emerge. I have had a very profound "glyph moment" using the cellular repair glyph. I had a clearing of sadness and grief through the use of this glyph. I think that it is through the encoding of healing the affliction, that cleared this for me. I have been carrying this for ten years now, and I know it is gone. Thank you so much!

Rev Barbara Ross

My friend, Janice, was very distressed late one evening because her beloved dog, Abby, was in pain and unable to lie down, eat or do anything other than stand next to Janice and shake. She had decided to take her to the vet in the morning with the realization that Abby would likely have to be put to sleep as it appeared Abby had a kidney disease.

There had been a previous occurrence with the vet letting Janice know that Abby would probably not make it if the problem persisted. I had Janice download Unlocking the Power of Glyphs and print Glyph 04-Detoxification. She gingerly placed a block of the glyphs on Abby and one under Abby after getting her to lie down (she appeared to be in pain so this had to be done very gently). Janice also put a few drops of Peace & Calming Essential oil blend on the pads of Abby's paws.

After about an hour, Abby got up and went in the kitchen to drink water; her tail was up and perky again after being droopy and tucked under her body. When she woke up in the morning after a night with the glyphs, Abby returned to normal eating and drinking. She was fine and able to go out for a walk. That night I tested Abby using my pendulum and found there were parasites in the kidney area. Janice began working with the Parasite Glyph, and amusingly, Abby began administering her own program as she would lay on the glyph for a half an hour and then move to another spot. Soon she would return to the glyph, and this pattern persisted for the evening. Two weeks later, Abby is still fine, but the glyph is still in her doggy bed.

Sakara Kemilla

Margie's cat had been urinating on the bed, Margie's clothing and anything else the cat could find to wet on. This had been going on for several weeks and had become a serious problem. When we examined a photograph of the room, there appeared to be several non-physical presences in the room. By dowsing with a pendulum we decided to place the #61 Entity Glyph in each of the four corners of the room and one in the center of the room. The cat began playing a stalking game with the images on the Glyphs - pouncing on them, slapping at the image with her paw and then stalking backwards still keeping her eyes focused on the Glyph. It was quite comical to observe her. After four days of leaving the Glyphs on the floor, the cat had stopped urinating on the bedding and clothing. The presences are also no longer detectable in the photos, through dowsing or by "intuitive sight." Thank goodness this cat and her owner will be able to remain roommates! Additionally, Margie is sleeping much better in the bedroom and says she feels generally better since the "treatment" on the room.

Sakara Kemilla

Appendix E

Resolving Brain Damage – Jessie's Story

In 2004 my husband Dean and I adopted Jessie, a black mixed breed dog from the local shelter. She was approximately three years old at the time. We got her to be a companion for our hound, Roscoe.

Roscoe was delighted with the playful companionship of Jessie; however, one problem we immediately encountered with her was car sickness. Every time we drove even a short distance, she would get car sick. Flower remedies which were helpful with other dogs, were ineffective. As I was working with empowering symbols and glyphs, I started out to design one that would balance her equilibrium. This was no help. I designed another one to emulate the frequency of a popular over-the-counter sea sickness medication. I had been successful in duplicating the energy of different medications or herbs with glyphs on previous occasions. If the glyph stayed on Jessie, as I held her in my lap, it seemed to help, but when I put her in the back with Roscoe, she would pull it off and start throwing up again. In total frustration I finally asked for guidance. (When will I ever learn to ask for guidance first?) I asked Source for help. I received the answer that Jesse had suffered brain damage from starvation and dehydration as a puppy. I was told she could be helped by creating a glyph designed to rebuild the area of her brain that was not developed normally. I was also told I must know the part of her brain that needed help to put in the wording of the glyph. I then asked "How should I get that, dowse?" The answer I received was, "You could but I will tell you if you ask." A good lesson here was the importance of asking for the information we want. Whenever we ask, we will always receive the answer. I replied, "I am asking." I received a reply that the brain part that needed restoration was the cerebellum. I then created a glyph to regenerate the undeveloped cerebellum and empowered it. Dean scanned the glyph, cataloged it, designed the master catalog header, and made patches to put on the dog. In the evening before she went to sleep, I taped the glyph on her crown chakra, which is right at the top of her head between the ears. The look on her face showed me that she was feeling something strange going on but she had no problem going to sleep. The glyphs are never painful but do sometimes cause a sensation of something happening inside the body. We put the glyph on every night for two weeks. After this two-week period we noticed a considerable improvement in her car sickness but still had an occasional occurrence of throwing up when riding on a winding mountain road. We then used the glyph on her for another two weeks. It has now been more than five years and Jessie has never had another problem with car sickness. I want to point out that animals are not skeptics, they do not wonder how long it is going to take and they are not disappointed when it does not work fast enough, therefore there is no resistant energy getting in the way of healing. It would be interesting to see if this glyph could help football players with traumatic encephalopathy, which can be fatal.

We must proceed with caution regarding changing people without first asking permission. I have a nephew who is retarded. I initially thought that perhaps I could help him. When I asked I was informed that I must not interfere. He had chosen to be as he is and does not desire any help. In cases like this, we must resist the temptation to "fix" someone and honor their path. It will take some further research to see how far we can take this ability, but we must proceed with caution.

Appendix F

Assistance Program for Children

Children are the Future

We are helping them get from here…

All over the world there are children sleeping in streets, doorways and under cardboard boxes, surviving by eating leftover food, doing heavy manual labor, selling trinkets, begging and stealing. Children are the future of their country, and of the world. One step at a time they can be helped to believe in their ability to create a better life for themselves and their community. It is not our goal to change their spiritual beliefs, only to help them realize how wonderful and powerful they are and that they can make a difference. A good example is an orphanage in Nepal that *Holy Ground Farm* is assisting.

100% of all donations are used to support programs for children.

To here.

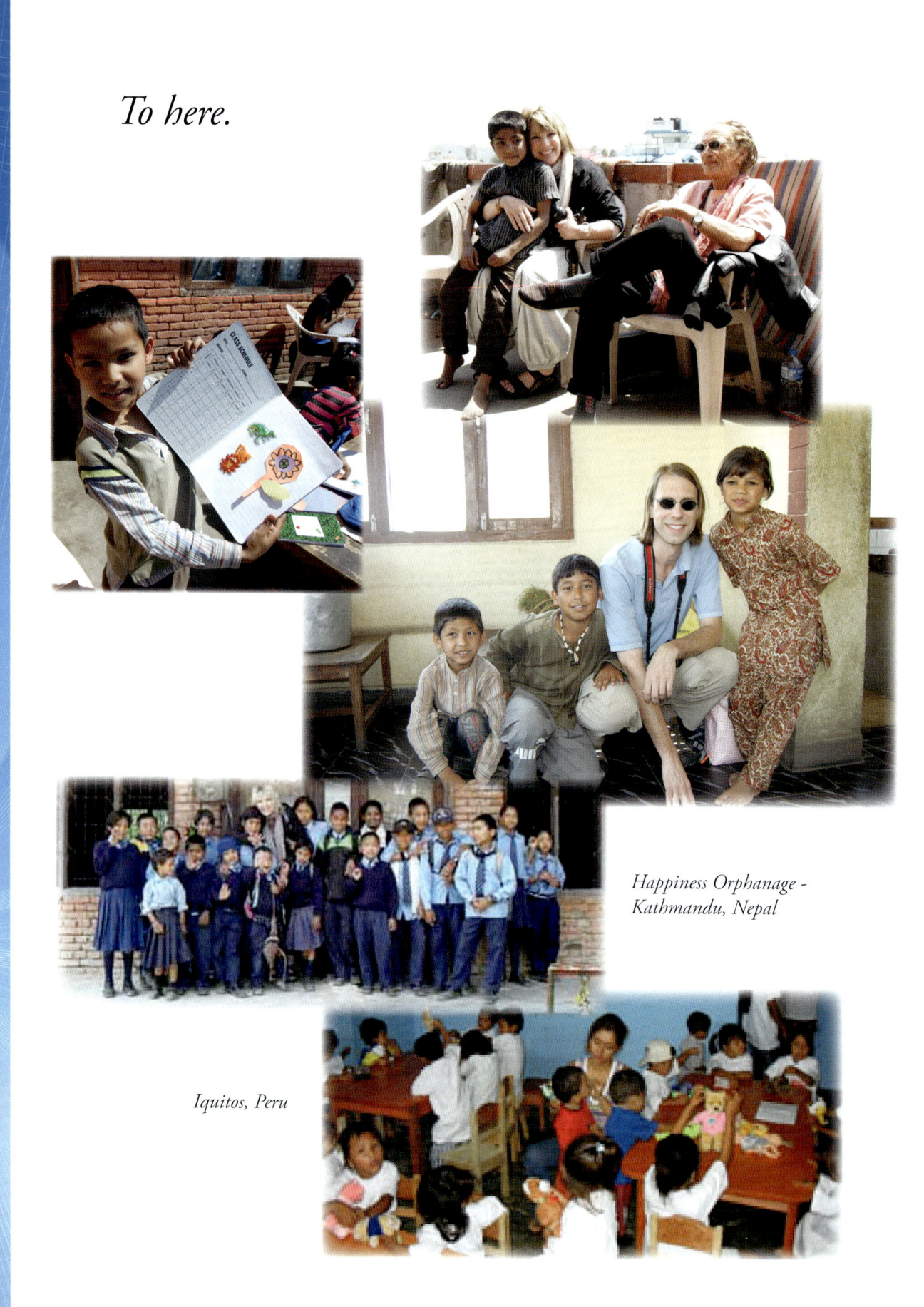

Happiness Orphanage -
Kathmandu, Nepal

Iquitos, Peru

Appendix G

Suggested Resources

Marciniak, Barbara
> ***Bringers of the Dawn***, Bear & Company, 1992.
> ***Path of Empowerment***, New World Library, 2004

Patricia, Cori
> ***The Cosmos of Soul,*** A Wake-Up Call for Humanity
> North Atlantic Books, 2000
> ***Atlantis Rising***, The Struggle of Darkness and Light
> North Atlantic Books, 2001
> ***No More Secrets, No More L***ies, A Handbook to Starseed Awakening
> North Atlantic Books, 2000

Louise L. Hay
> ***Heal Your Body***, The Mental Causes for Physical Illness
> and the Metaphysical Way to Overcome Them, Hay House, 1982
> ***Experience Your Good Now!*** Learning to Use Affirmations
> Hay House, 2010

Silva, Freddy
> ***Secrets in the Fields***, The Science and Mysticism of Crop
> Circles, Hampton Roads Publishing, 2002

Hawkins, David
> ***Power vs Force***, The Hidden Determinants of Human
> Behavior, Hay House, 1995

Emoto, Masaru
> ***The Hidden Messages in Water***, Beyond Words Publishing, 2004

Peggy Black
> ***"We Are Here" Transmissions, the Morning Messages*** book and CD

Appendix H

This is a reading for Jean Logan by Judith Moore - 2004

"There is a new language of Light that is to come on to the planet. It is an organization of Light particles that is encoded in the vibrations you are bringing through your glyphs. Your glyphs are emanating frequencies into the Light fields of the planet. You are a being from the higher realms. You have entered the earth body from the source of the masters and you carry the master code. The master code is what has guided you and the master code is what directs you now…….Throughout the history of humanity on this planet you have been present during peaks of enlightened consciousness. You are of the House of the Masters. When you were sent to earth, the temple of the masters was sent to earth for you to create the language of the masters here on earth. These masters are the masters of Divine Light………. when the next renaissance of consciousness is almost ready, you and others like you come in with the master code to facilitate the organization of light so that there is an availability for a broader spectrum of vibrational energy on the planet that facilitates leaps in consciousness and renaissance………The language that you are bringing right now is a language that will organize the atmospheric particles to facilitate an expansion of the prismatic fields, and the expansion of the way we use light…"

"You have everything to do with facilitating human consciousness in being able to utilize these light fields because you carry the master code. I am being guided to journey to the realm of the masters together……….."

"As you are opening up I am seeing an image of the Peruvian mountains. I am seeing star brothers. UFOs come through a stargate into the mountain. I am seeing you as a Peruvian Indian and as you are carrying a staff and climbing the mountain, you see these starships as balls of Light that go through into the mountain. You climb the mountain and stand in front of the gateway where the starships went into the mountain in Peru. From the gateway came a beam of light, almost like a laser… opening up your master code, code of Light and you are activated in that life time as a light bearer. You came down from the mountain and assisted in building Machu Picchu. In Machu Picchu you placed lenses that would receive the sun rays that would refract the light. Your guides are telling me to go back to that portal in Peru…"

"She went through the pineal gland portal at the anterior lobe of her pineal gland back to Machu Picchu and to ascending the mountain top where she saw light ships going through a portal and a beam of light came out and struck her and she was pulled in through the portal and when she went in she experienced beings so brilliant that normal eyes could not see them.… I see you there being taken to an ancient….tablet and I see you sit before the tablet and you send a beam of light from your third eye to each of the glyphs that are on the tablet. And as you do that you are downloaded from the tablet. The glyph comes in through your third eye and into your pineal gland and then it is downloaded into your energy field. I am seeing the light beings stand around you and tone and chant a very high pitched chant. When you are finished with one tablet, and these tablets are about three or four feet high and there are nine ancient tablets of the Peruvian Light bearers. I am being told these are the tablets of Pacal Votan. As you are in this mystical cavern, in this mystical realm, you are connecting to the light beings that carry the soul codes that you carry for illuminating the light frequencies and assisting humanity in the leap of consciousness. ….. you receive these ancient encodements from the tablets in South America by Machu Picchu."

"You have in many lifetimes carried the light of hope and illuminated the darkness. Never underestimate the power of the hope that you carry or the power of your Light once it is given permission to act and work in your life for the unfolding of your divine purpose…..Where ever your physical genetic lineage comes from you are in a lineage of the light bearers that came to earth… You have extraterrestrial DNA."

"When I looked at your DNA I saw a filament of light in your DNA that most people do not have. So that is connected with this ability. That filament of light is connected with this ability to bring through that light language. When you can conceive that the glyphs don't just work on the DNA, the DNA projects information based on its ability to receive and project light. When you think of it in terms of a holographic field, then you can understand that the glyphs that you are bringing in actually help bring high vibration light fields. The light fields helps resolve the dense energy that is light starved."

Appendix I

Disclaimer

The glyphs in this book represent the power of prayer. They should not be construed as orthodox or alternative medicine, diagnostic tools, or medical devices for the treatment of any type of disease or illness. The prayer energy from the glyphs helps enable the user to heal themselves, which is their right to do. These glyphs should not replace or interfere with any type of medical treatment. In the case of any serious illness, always consult a qualified medical practitioner.

RISING STARS ASSESSMENT

Science Progress Tests

Year 6

Pauline Hannigan
Series Advisors: Cornwall Learning

RISING STARS

CORNWALL LEARNING

Rising Stars UK Ltd, 7 Hatchers Mews, Bermondsey Street, London SE1 3GS

www.risingstars-uk.com

First published 2014

Text, design and layout © Rising Stars UK Ltd 2014

The right of Pauline Hannigan to be identified as the author of this work has been asserted by her in accordance with the Copyright, Design and Patents Act 1998.

Some material based on Rising Stars Assessment Science Unit Tests Years 5–6
© Rising Stars 2008

All facts are correct at time of going to press.

Author: Pauline Hannigan
Educational consultant: Ed Walsh, Cornwall Learning
Accessibility reviewer: Vivien Kilburn
Editorial: Susan Gardner, David Mantovani and Lynette Woodward
Typist: Rosalyn Dale
Design: Ray Rich and Clive Sutherland
Illustrations: Oxford Designers and Illustrators
Photos: istockphoto.com
Cover design: Burville-Riley Partnership

Rising Stars is grateful to the following people and schools who contributed to the development of these materials.
Plumcroft Primary School, London; Rainford Brook Lodge Primary School, Merseyside; St Nicholas CE Primary School, Chislehurst; St Margaret's CE Primary School, Heywood, Rochdale; Tennyson Road Primary School, Luton

All rights reserved. No part of this publication may be reproduced, stored in a retrieval system, or transmitted, in any form by any means, electronic, mechanical, photocopying, recording or otherwise, without the prior permission of Rising Stars.

British Library Cataloguing in Publication Data.
A CIP record for this book is available from the British Library.
ISBN: 978 1 84680 965 1

MIX
Paper from responsible sources
FSC® C011748

Printed by Ashford Colour Press

Contents

Introduction	4
Pupil progress sheet	8
Living things and their habitats	**9**
Test 1 (diagnostic assessment)	9
Test 2 (mid-topic)	12
Test 3 (end of topic)	14
Test 4 (end of year)	16
Animals, including humans	**18**
Test 1 (diagnostic assessment)	18
Test 2 (mid-topic)	20
Test 3 (end of topic)	22
Test 4 (end of year)	24
Evolution and inheritance	**27**
Test 1 (diagnostic assessment)	27
Test 2 (mid-topic)	29
Test 3 (end of topic)	31
Test 4 (end of year)	34
Light	**36**
Test 1 (diagnostic assessment)	36
Test 2 (mid-topic)	39
Test 3 (end of topic)	41
Test 4 (end of year)	43
Electricity	**46**
Test 1 (diagnostic assessment)	46
Test 2 (mid-topic)	48
Test 3 (end of topic)	50
Test 4 (end of year)	52
Answers and mark schemes	54

Introduction

Why use Rising Stars Assessment Progress Tests?

The *Rising Stars Assessment Science Progress Tests* have been developed to support teachers assess the progress their pupils are making against the 2014 National Curriculum Programme of Study for science. The tests are designed to support effective classroom assessment across Years 1 to 6 and are easy to use and mark.

The tests are organised around the topics in the Programme of Study and have been:
- written by primary science assessment specialists
- reviewed by primary science curriculum and assessment experts.

How do the tests track progress?

The results data from the tests can be used to track progress. They show whether pupils are making the expected progress for their year, more than expected progress or less than expected progress. This data can then be used alongside other evidence to enable effective planning of future teaching and learning, for reporting to parents and as evidence for Ofsted inspections. If teachers are using the CD-ROM version of the tests, the results data can be keyed into the Progress Tracker (see page 7 for more information), which automatically shows the progress of individual pupils against the Programme of Study and the results for all pupils by question and test. Data can also be exported into the school's management information system (MIS).

About the Science Progress Tests

The tests are written to match the content requirements of the Programme of Study for the 2014 National Curriculum. The content areas are:

Content	Year 1	Year 2	Year 3	Year 4	Year 5	Year 6
Living things (and their habitats)		✓		✓	✓	✓
Plants	✓	✓	✓			
Animals, including humans	✓	✓	✓	✓	✓	✓
Evolution and inheritance						✓
Materials (uses, properties and changes)	✓	✓			✓	
Rocks			✓			
States of matter				✓		
Light			✓			✓
Sound				✓		
Seasonal changes/Earth and space	✓				✓	
Forces (and magnets)			✓		✓	
Electricity				✓		✓

In line with the Programme of Study, the skills of working scientifically are assessed through all the content areas rather than separately. For each content area there are four tests:
- Test 1 (diagnostic) – note that for Years 1 and 2 this is a checklist rather than a test to make it more accessible and informative for pupils whose written language skills are likely to be less developed

Year 6 Introduction

- Test 2 (mid-topic)
- Test 3 (end of topic)
- Test 4 (end of year)

The marks for each test are as follows:

Test	Number of marks						
	Year 1	Year 2	Year 3	Year 4	Year 5	Year 6
Test/Checklist 1 (diagnostic)	N/A	N/A	10	10	10	10
Test 2 (mid-topic)	10	10	10	10	10	10
Test 3 (end of topic)	10	10	10	10	10	10
Test 4 (end of year)	10	10	10	10	10	10

Test demand

The first test for each topic is designed to help teachers assess the prior learning of individual pupils and the class before teaching begins. These tests/checklists are more open-ended than tests 2–4 to elicit as much information as possible to help teachers refine their plans for teaching the topic.

Test 2 is designed to be used during a topic, test 3 at the end of a topic and test 4 at the end of the year. Test 4 could optionally be used as an alternative or additional test at the end of a topic. Tests 2–4 follow the same approach. In each test:

- 5 marks are allocated to knowledge and understanding
- 5 marks are allocated to application
- 4 marks additionally assess working scientifically.

Tests 2–4 also contain a mix of objective questions and questions requiring written answers.

Tracking progress

The marks pupils score in the tests can be used to track how they are progressing against the expected outcomes for their year group in relation to the National Curriculum Programme of Study. The marks for tests 2–4 for each topic have been split into three progress zones:

- less than expected progress
- expected progress
- more than expected progress.

The zones for each year group are as follows:

		Zone mark range		
	Test	Less than expected progress	Expected progress	More than expected progress
Year 1	2–4	0–5	6–8	9–10
Year 2	2–4	0–5	6–8	9–10
Year 3	2–4	0–5	6–8	9–10
Year 4	2–4	0–5	6–8	9–10
Year 5	2–4	0–5	6–8	9–10
Year 6	2–4	0–5	6–8	9–10

The table gives the mark ranges for the progress zones for each test which you can use to see how well each pupil is doing in each test. If pupils are making the expected progress for their

Year 6 Introduction

year they will be consistently scoring marks in the middle zone of marks in the tests. The higher the mark in the zone, the more secure you can be that they are making expected progress.

Determining prior learning

The first test for each topic is provided to help teachers find out about prior learning.

For Years 1 and 2 these tests are in the form of diagnostic checklists to enable an oral investigation of prior learning as it is recognised that pupils have limited reading and writing vocabularies, particularly in Year 1. Each checklist comprises a set of questions to ask pupils and supporting visual prompts. There is also a Pupil Responses Form that can be used to record whether some, most or all pupils are able to answer each question.

For Years 3–6 there is a diagnostic test for each topic. These tests can be administered as described below and the marks analysed to identify the prior learning of individual pupils and the class as a whole.

How to use the Science Progress Tests

Preparation and timings

1 Make enough copies of the test(s) for each pupil to have their own copy.
2 Hand out the papers and ensure pupils are seated appropriately so that they can't see each other's papers.
3 Pupils will need pens or pencils, rulers and erasers. Encourage pupils to cross out answers rather than rub them out.
4 There are no time limits for the tests but normal practice is to allow a minute per mark for written tests. Help with reading may be given using the same rules as when providing a reader with the DfE KS2 tests.

Supporting pupils during the tests

Before the test explain to the pupils that the test is an opportunity to show what they know, understand and can do. They should try to answer all the questions but should not worry if there are some they can't do.

Many pupils will be able to work independently in the tests, with minimal support from the teacher or a teaching assistant. However, pupils should be encouraged to 'have a go' at a question, or to move on to a fresh question if they appear to be stuck, to ensure that no pupil becomes distressed.

It is important that pupils receive appropriate support, but are not unfairly advantaged or disadvantaged. Throughout the tests, therefore, the teacher may read, explain or sign to a pupil any parts of the test that include instructions, for example by demonstrating how to circle an answer.

With younger age groups you may also consider using the version of the test on the CD-ROM and projecting it on to a whiteboard to support a whole class or group to take the tests. You may choose to refer to the words on the whiteboard and read them aloud so that pupils can follow them on the screen and on their own test paper and then write their answers on their papers individually.

Marking the tests

Use the detailed mark scheme and your professional judgement to award marks. **Do not award half marks.**

It is useful to use peer marking of test questions from time to time. Pupils should exchange test sheets and mark them as you read out the question and answer. You will need to check that pupils are marking accurately. This approach also provides an opportunity to recap on any questions that pupils found difficult to answer.

Feeding back to pupils

Once the test has been marked, use a five-minute feedback session with the pupils to help them review their answers. Wherever possible pupils should be encouraged to make their own corrections as in this way they will become more aware of their own strengths and weaknesses. Agree with each pupil what they did well in the test and what the targets are for them to improve. A template Pupil Progress Sheet is provided on page 8 for this purpose.

Using the Progress Tracker

The second table on page 5 gives the mark ranges for the progress zones for each test, which you can use to see how well each pupil is doing in each test and across each topic. If pupils are making the expected progress for their year they will be consistently scoring marks in the middle zone of marks in the tests. The higher the mark in the zone, the more secure you can be that they are making expected progress.

The CD-ROM* version of *Science Progress Tests* includes an interactive Progress Tracker, which allows you to enter the marks for each question for each test by pupil. This then automatically shows you which zone the pupil is in and also the zone distribution for the class so that you can track the progress of individual pupils and the whole class.

The Progress Tracker also enables you to review the marks for each question so that you can identify areas where some or all pupils may need further support and areas where some or all pupils are ready to be stretched further. It also provides a separate summary of marks for each pupil for knowledge and understanding, application, and working scientifically so that you can identify if pupils have strengths or weaknesses in a particular area.

If required, data from the tests can be exported into the school's management information system (MIS) so that it can be used alongside other data in whole school monitoring including the monitoring of specific groups of pupils, such as Pupil Premium.

Full details about the Progress Tracker are provided on the CD-ROM.

* If you have the book version only of *Science Progress Tests*, the Progress Tracker can be downloaded from bit.ly/progtracker

Pupil progress sheet

Name: _____ Class: _____ Date: _____

Topic name: _____ Test number: _____ My mark: _____

What I did well in the test:

_____

_____

_____

What I need to do to improve:

1. _____

2. _____

3. _____

✂ -

Pupil progress sheet

Name: _____ Class: _____ Date: _____

Topic name: _____ Test number: _____ My mark: _____

What I did well in the test:

_____

_____

_____

What I need to do to improve:

1. _____

2. _____

3. _____

© Rising Stars UK Ltd 2014.   You may photocopy this page.

Year 6
Living things and their habitats Test 1 (diagnostic)

Name: _____ Class: _____ Date: _____

1.

ant spider centipede

worm beetle slug

Sam found some animals in his garden. He sorted them into two groups. What **two** groups could he have chosen?

i) _____

ii) _____

A/WS

1 mark

2. Use arrows to sort the animals into two groups.

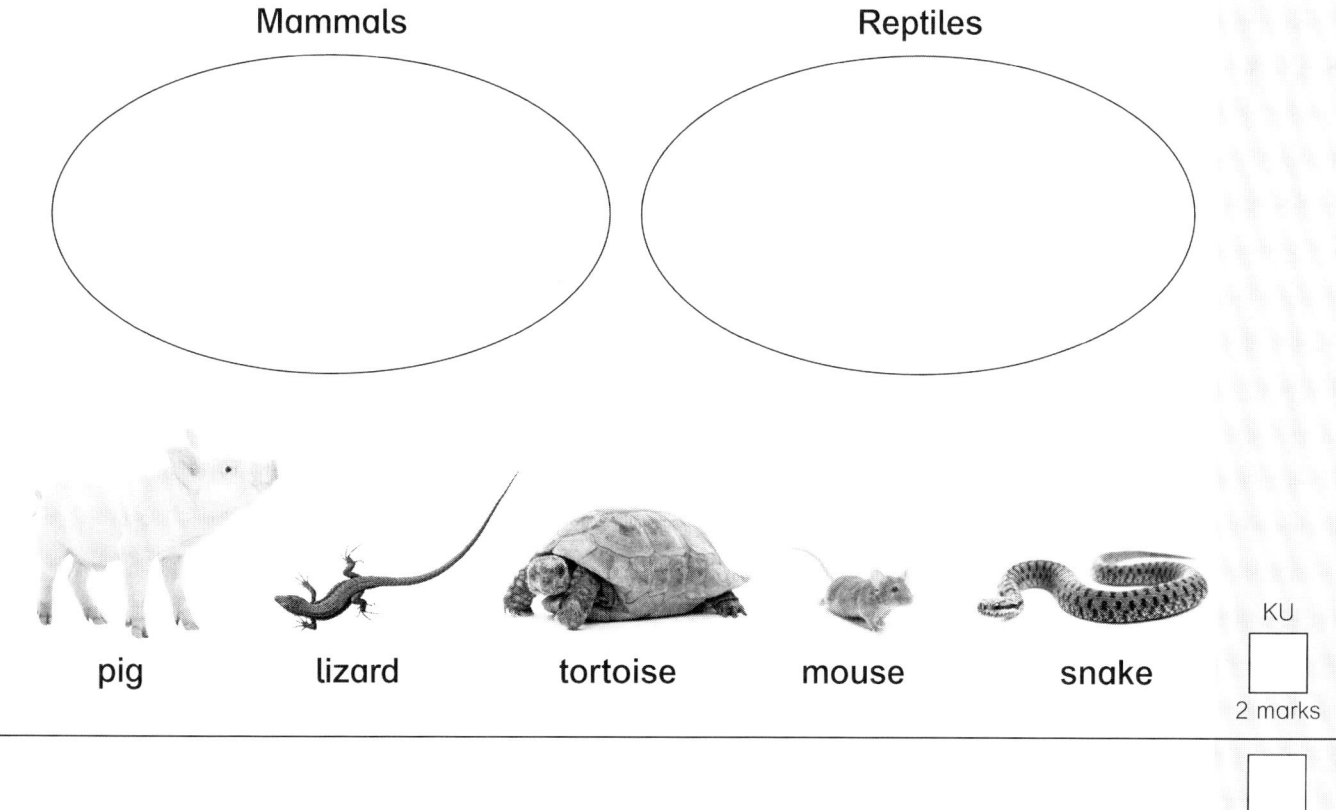

Mammals   Reptiles

pig   lizard   tortoise   mouse   snake

KU

2 marks

Total for this page

Year 6 **Living things and their habitats** Test 1 (diagnostic)

3. a) A key is used to sort these flowering plants.

   Choose **two** questions from the following list and write each one in the correct box in the key.
   - Do the petals stand upright?
   - Are the petals large and round?
   - Are the flowers single?

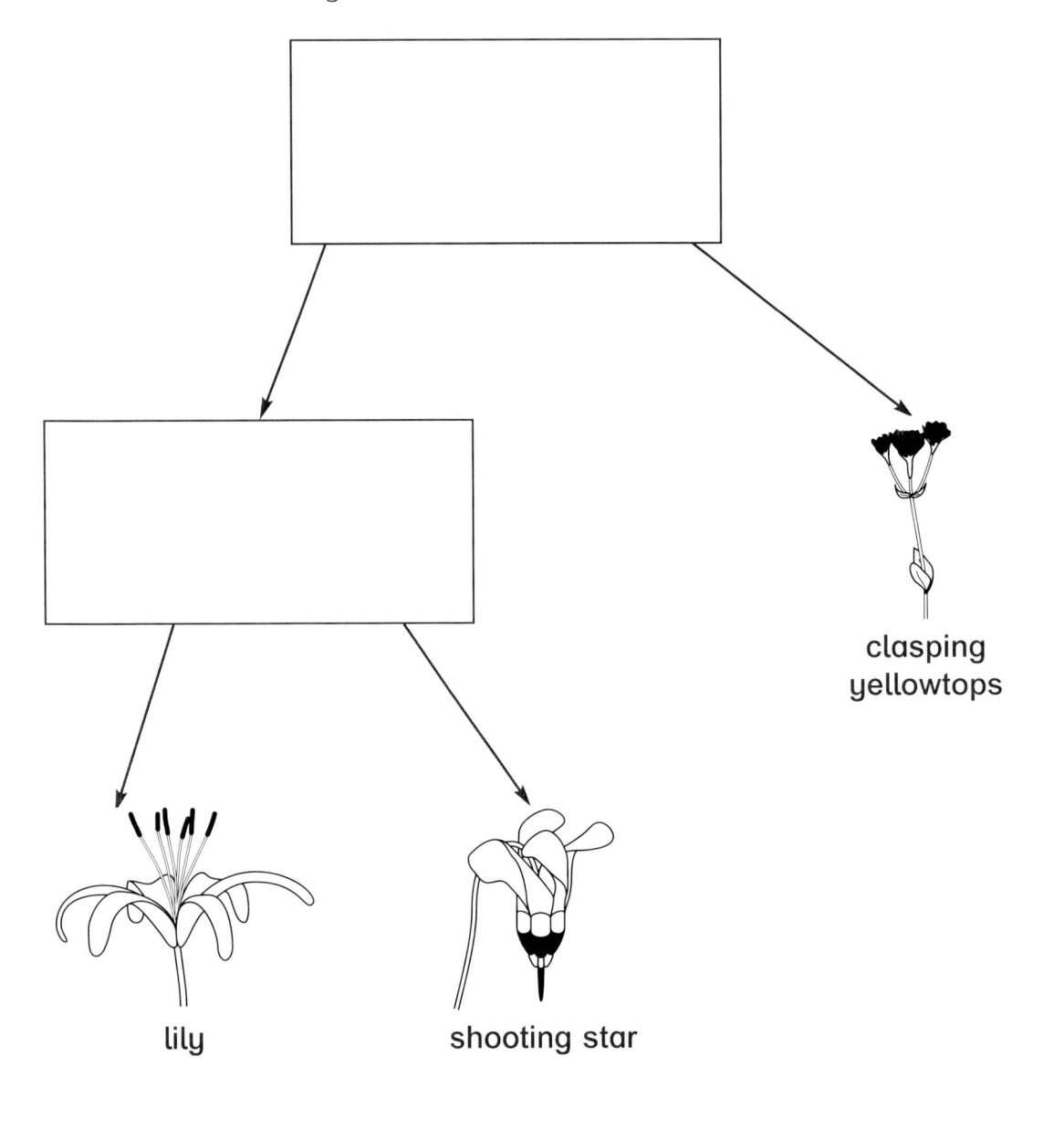

   clasping yellowtops

   lily

   shooting star

   b) Write YES and NO in the correct places in the key.

   c) Give **one** reason why a key is useful.

4. Give **two** good uses of micro-organisms.

2 marks

5. Look at the chart.

Give **one** piece of evidence that yeast is living.

	Yeast	Yeast and sugar
Start		
After two hours		

1 mark

Year 6
Living things and their habitats Test 2 (mid-topic)

Name: _____ Class: _____ Date: _____

1. Animals can be divided into two groups: animals that have backbones and animals that do not have backbones.

   What is the name of the group of animals with backbones?

   _____

   KU ☐ 1 mark

2. a) Draw arrows to put each animal in its correct group.

   | mammal | bird | amphibian | reptile | fish |

   swan   cod   dog   snake   frog

   A/WS ☐ 2 marks

   b) Which group would a kangaroo go in?

   _____

   A/WS ☐ 1 mark

   c) Give **one** reason for your answer to part **b**.

   _____

   A/WS ☐ 1 mark

Total for this page ☐

12 © Rising Stars UK Ltd 2014. You may photocopy this page.

d) Tick **two** features that all reptiles have in common.

☐ They lay eggs in water.

☐ They give birth to live young.

☐ They are cold blooded.

☐ They have scaly skin.

☐ They have legs.

KU

2 marks

3. Give **two** reasons why scientists use keys when they are studying plants and animals.

KU

2 marks

4. Give **one bad** effect of micro-organisms.

A

1 mark

/10
Total for this test

Year 6
Living things and their habitats Test 3 (end of topic)

Name: _____ Class: _____ Date: _____

1. a) Class 6 were researching different types of animals.

They found that animals can be divided into two groups: animals that have backbones and animals that do not have backbones.

What is the name of the group that do **not** have backbones?

_____

b) Class 6 collected some animals from the school garden.

Give **one** reason why they only found animals **without** backbones.

_____

c) The children made a key to sort the animals they found.

```
                    ┌─────────────────┐
                    │ A _____ │
                    └─────────────────┘
                   YES/NO      YES/NO
                    ↙              ↘
        ┌─────────────────┐    ┌─────────────────┐
        │ B _____ │    │ C _____ │
        └─────────────────┘    └─────────────────┘
         YES/NO   YES/NO         YES/NO   YES/NO
          ↓         ↓              ↓         ↓
        ladybird  spider          slug     snail
```

Look at this list of questions:

Does it have wings?   Does it have legs?   Does it have six legs?

i) Choose the question the children wrote in box A and write it in box A.

ii) Choose the question the children wrote in box B and write it in box B.

KU — 1 mark
A — 1 mark
KU — 1 mark
KU — 1 mark

Total for this page

14   © Rising Stars UK Ltd 2014.   You may photocopy this page.

d) Think of a good question for box C.

Write it on the key.

e) Look at the YES/NO arrows on the key.

Circle YES or NO so that the key is correct.

f) Think of **one** different animal that the children could have found.

Write the name of this animal in the correct place on the key.

2. Give **two** good uses of micro-organisms.

Year 6
Living things and their habitats Test 4 (end of year)

Name: _____ Class: _____ Date: _____

1. Name **two** features of a plant that make it different from an animal.

   ....

   ....

   KU
   2 marks

2. a) Tick the **one** that is true.

   ☐ A fungus is a special type of plant.

   ☐ A fungus is an animal.

   ☐ A fungus is neither a plant nor an animal.

   KU
   1 mark

   b) Circle the one that is **not** a fungus.

   seaweed   mould   yeast   mushroom

   KU
   1 mark

   c) Name **one** way in which fungi are different from plants.

   ....

   KU
   1 mark

3. Give **one** reason why a lizard is **not** an amphibian.

   ....

   A
   1 mark

   Total for this page

16   © Rising Stars UK Ltd 2014.   You may photocopy this page.

Year 6 Living things and their habitats Test 4 (end of year)

4. a) Becky is testing how much mould grows on strawberries at different temperatures.

Write down **one** thing that Becky needs to keep the same to help her make her test fair.

....

A/WS

1 mark

b) Draw arrows to match each of these strawberries with the temperature at which it was stored for one week.

| 8°C | 2°C | 15°C |

A/WS

2 marks

c) What conclusion can Becky draw from this investigation of temperature and growth of mould on strawberries?

....

....

A/WS

1 mark

/10

Total for this test

Year 6
Animals, including humans Test 1 (diagnostic)

Name: _____ Class: _____ Date: _____

1. **a)** Draw an X on the diagram to show where the heart is.

KU ☐ 1 mark

   b) What does the heart do?

   _____

KU ☐ 1 mark

   c) Why does your heart beat faster during exercise?

   _____
   _____

KU ☐ 1 mark

2. **a)** Tick the foods that are important for a balanced diet.

KU ☐ 1 mark

   b) Why do you need to eat a balanced diet?

   _____

A ☐ 1 mark

3. **a)** Give **one** reason why it is important to exercise.

   _____

A ☐ 1 mark

   b) *If you exercise you do not need to eat a balanced diet.* — Ali

   Is Ali right?

   yes ☐   no ☐

KU ☐ 1 mark

Total for this page ☐

18

© Rising Stars UK Ltd 2014.   You may photocopy this page.

4. **a)** A group of children in Class 6 are investigating what happens to their pulse rates after they have done 100 star jumps.

They draw a table of their results.

	Pulse rate per minute		
	Before jumps	Straight after jumps	After 5 minutes' rest
Carly	88	125	90
Matt	95	130	94
Amy	98	136	99
Ben	90	135	95

Whose pulse rate has gone up most after the star jumps?

....

b) Carly says that most people's pulse rate goes back to normal after 5 minutes' rest?

Is Carly right?

yes ☐   no ☐

c) Give **one** reason why the children's results might not be accurate.

....
....

Year 6
Animals, including humans Test 2 (mid-topic)

Name: _____ Class: _____ Date: _____

1. a) Tick **one** thing that the blood transports around the body.

   food ☐

   air ☐

   oxygen ☐

   b) What is the job of the heart?

   _____

   c) What is your pulse?

   _____

2. Circle the name of the vessel that does **not** carry blood around the body.

   oesophagus   artery   capillary   vein

3. **a)** Tom drew a graph of his pulse rate during a PE lesson.

Tom's pulse rate

[Graph showing pulse rate (beats per minute) on y-axis from 0 to 120, and Time of day (p.m.) on x-axis from 1:00 to 2:00. Points labelled: A at 1:10, 80 bpm; B at 1:15, 110 bpm; C at 1:45, 110 bpm; D at 1:55, 80 bpm.]

Tick the time that Tom started to exercise.

☐ 1:00   ☐ 1:05   ☐ 1:10   ☐ 1:15

1 mark

b) Give **one** other change Tom could have noticed in his body during the PE lesson.

....

1 mark

c) What happened to Tom's pulse rate between points C and D on the graph?

....

1 mark

d) Why did this happen?

....

1 mark

e) Tom repeated his investigation during the next PE lesson. Tick the reason he did this.

☐ To make his test fair.   ☐ To check his results are reliable.

1 mark

4. When is it all right to take drugs?

....

1 mark

/10

Total for this test

Year 6
Animals, including humans Test 3 (end of topic)

Name: _____ Class: _____ Date: _____

1. a) Draw arrows from the foods to put them in the correct groups.

   | pasta | salmon | eggs | rice | bread | chicken |

   Carbohydrates   Protein

   2 marks

   b) Give **one** reason why it is important to eat plenty of protein.

   _____

   1 mark

2. Two hundred years ago, ships could not store fruit and vegetables and because of this sailors often got a disease called scurvy. Why?

   _____
   _____

   1 mark

3. a) Jamie and his friends noticed how they got out of breath when they ran fast. They set up an investigation. Here are the results.

Breathing rate per minute		
	At rest	After running 50 m
Jamie	15	40
Zara	18	38
Bess	13	43
Jack	16	44

What question were they trying to answer?

_____

b) Circle the name of the person whose breathing rate went up the most.

    Jamie   Zara   Bess   Jack

c) Explain why the children's breathing got faster.

_____

_____

d) Zara said they should repeat their investigation because their results might not have been accurate.

Tick **two** reasons why their results might not have been accurate.

☐ It is difficult to count breathing rate.

☐ Heart rate increases after exercise.

☐ It is possible to make yourself breathe more slowly.

4. Give **two** possible side effects of smoking tobacco.

_____

_____

Year 6
Animals, including humans Test 4 (end of year)

Name: _____ Class: _____ Date: _____

1. Megan is eating a sandwich.
Put numbers in the boxes to show how the nutrients from the sandwich travel through Megan's body to reach her muscles.
One has been done for you.

[ ] blood

[1] mouth

[ ] muscles

[ ] small intestine

[ ] stomach

KU
2 marks

2. Sugar is a good source of energy.
Name **one** thing that could happen if you eat too much sugar.

_____

KU
1 mark

3. Write **one** thing that happens to the blood in the lungs.

_____

KU
1 mark

Total for this page

24 © Rising Stars UK Ltd 2014. You may photocopy this page.

4. **a)** This graph shows the number of deaths from lung cancer in the UK since 1990.

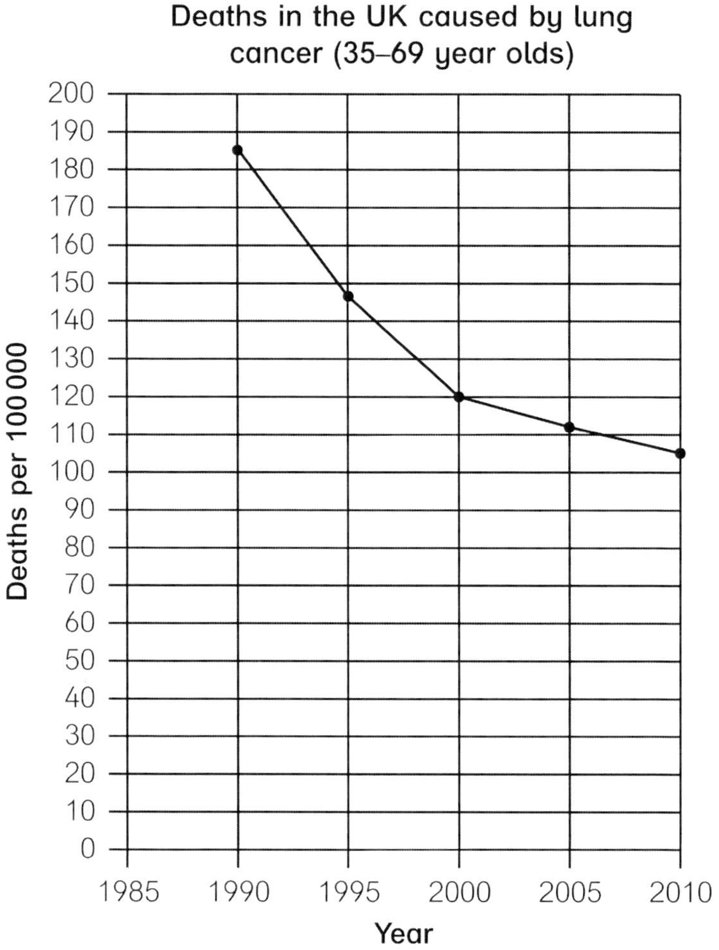
Deaths in the UK caused by lung cancer (35–69 year olds)
Deaths per 100 000
200
190
180
170
160
150
140
130
120
110
100
90
80
70
60
50
40
30
20
10
0
1985
1990
1995
2000
2005
2010
Year

Have the number of deaths from lung cancer gone up or down since 1990?

Tick the correct answer.

☐ **gone up** ☐ **gone down**

A/WS ☐ 1 mark

b) Between which years was there the biggest change in the number of deaths?

Between .... and ....

A/WS ☐ 1 mark

c) What does this graph suggest about the number of people who smoke in the UK?

....

A/WS ☐ 1 mark

d) How could this idea be tested?

....

A/WS ☐ 1 mark

☐ Total for this page

Year 6 **Animals, including humans** Test 4 (end of year)

5. Write **one** reason why exercise is important.

_____

_____

_____

KU ☐ 1 mark

6. Tick **two** possible effects of getting drunk through drinking too much alcohol.

☐ make better decisions

☐ damaged liver

☐ think more clearly

☐ loss of control

A ☐ 1 mark

/10
Total for this test

Year 6
Evolution and inheritance Test 1 (diagnostic)

Name: _____ Class: _____ Date: _____

1. a) What is a fossil?

    _____

    KU
    1 mark

    b) How many years old are fossils? Circle the correct answer.

    millions   hundreds   thousands.

    KU
    1 mark

2. Fill in the missing word in this sentence.

    An animal or plant develops features over time that help it to live in its environment. This is called an _____

    KU
    1 mark

3. This is a sea bird called a cormorant.
    It dives under the water to catch fish.

    feet

    _____

    beak

    _____

    How do the cormorant's feet and beak help it to catch fish under water?
    Write your answers in the boxes.

    A
    2 marks

    Total for this page

© Rising Stars UK Ltd 2014. You may photocopy this page.

Year 6 Evolution and inheritance Test 1 (diagnostic)

4. a) This graph shows how the average height of men has changed between 1871 and 1975.

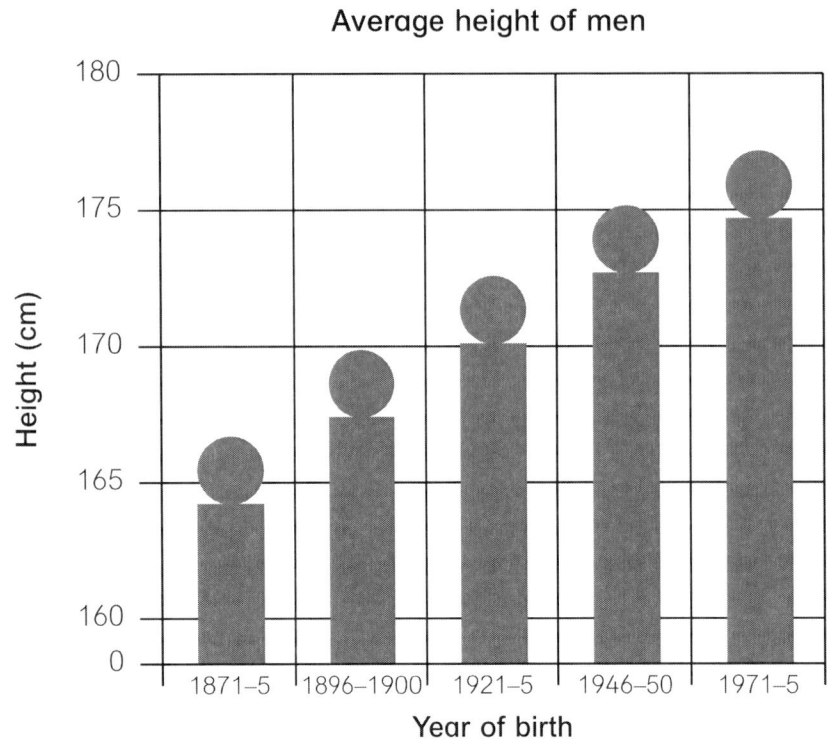

Average height of men

What does the graph show has happened to the average height of men during this time?

_____

A/WS
1 mark

b) About how much has the average height of men changed in 100 years?

Tick **one**.

☐ 5 cm   ☐ 10 cm   ☐ 15 cm   ☐ 20 cm

A/WS
1 mark

c) Tick **two** things that may have made the average height of men change during that time.

☐ They had a better diet.   ☐ There was less illness.

☐ They died at an older age.   ☐ They had more holidays.

A/WS
2 marks

5. Charlie has a pet cat with long white fur and a pointed nose. Why do you think the cat has those features?

_____

KU
1 mark

/10
Total for this test

Year 6
Evolution and inheritance Test 2 (mid-topic)

Name: _____ Class: _____ Date: _____

---

1. **a)** Here is a picture of an animal called a trilobite. It became extinct more than 250 million years ago.

How do we know it ever existed?

_____

KU [ ] 1 mark

b) How do scientists know how long ago it lived?

_____

_____

A [ ] 1 mark

---

2. Give **one** reason why animals become extinct.

_____

KU [ ] 1 mark

---

3. **a)** What are fossils?

_____

KU [ ] 1 mark

b) Tick how many years old the oldest fossils are.

[ ] 500 million

[ ] 5 million

[ ] 5 thousand

KU [ ] 1 mark

Total for this page [ ]

Year 6 **Evolution and inheritance** Test 2 (mid-topic)

4. a) Tick the name of a person who studies fossils.

☐ archaeologist   ☐ geologist   ☐ palaeontologist

KU / 1 mark

b) About 200 years ago Mary Anning found some fossilised bones from a creature now known as an ichthyosaurus. She thought they were from a crocodile.

Tick the **two** things she could have done to show her she was wrong.

☐ Found more bones

☐ Compared the bones she found to a picture of a crocodile

☐ Compared the bones she found to the skeleton of a crocodile

A/WS / 2 marks

c)

ichthyosaurus fossil

crocodile skeleton

Write **one** thing that is the **same** about the fossil of the ichthyosaurus and the skeleton of the crocodile.

_____

A/WS / 1 mark

d) Write **one** thing that is **different** about the fossil of the ichthyosaurus and the skeleton of the crocodile.

_____

A/WS / 1 mark

/10 **Total for this test**

© Rising Stars UK Ltd 2014. You may photocopy this page.

Year 6
Evolution and inheritance Test 3 (end of topic)

Name: _____ Class: _____ Date: _____

1. Jo and Becky are looking at a litter of puppies.

The puppies are similar, but not identical.

They all have the same parents.

a) How might the puppies vary?

_____

b) Suggest a feature that would have been passed on to the puppies from their parents.

_____

c) Suggest a feature that would have caused by the environment.

_____

Year 6 **Evolution and inheritance** Test 3 (end of topic)

2. Class 6 are discussing colour of eyes.

Amy: I think the environment affects the colour of your eyes.

Ben: It's passed on from your parents.

Abdul: I think it's affected by the environment AND passed on from your parents.

Charlene: I think it is just luck; it is completely random.

a) Who do you think is right?

_____

KU

1 mark

b) Explain why you decided this.

_____

KU

1 mark

Total for this page

Year 6   **Evolution and inheritance**   Test 3 (end of topic)

3. a) What does **adaptation** mean?

....

....

KU

1 mark

b) Tick **two** ways the cactus has adapted to living in hot dry climates.

☐ It has widespread roots.

☐ It has flowers.

☐ It can store water.

☐ It is eaten by some desert animals.

A/WS

2 marks

4. Scientists believe that humans have evolved into their present form over millions of years.

Give **two** ways humans have developed over time.

....

....

KU

2 marks

/10

Total for this test

© Rising Stars UK Ltd 2014. You may photocopy this page.

33

Year 6
Evolution and inheritance Test 4 (end of year)

Name: _____ Class: _____ Date: _____

1. a) Charles Darwin was a famous scientist. He studied birds called finches. He discovered that different finches had different shaped beaks, depending on what they ate.

   Class 6 did some research on other birds. This is a table of what they found.

Name of bird	Beak	What it eats
sparrow		
kestrel		
heron		
warbler		

   Look at the beaks of the birds in the table.
   Choose what each bird eats from the following list.
   Write your answers in the table:

       mice   insects   fish   seeds

   A/WS
   2 marks

   b) Explain why the children's research supported Darwin's findings.

   _____

   A/WS
   1 mark

   c) Owls eat rats and voles.
      What sort of beak would you expect an owl to have?

   _____

   A/WS
   1 mark

   Total for this page

© Rising Stars UK Ltd 2014. You may photocopy this page.

Year 6   **Evolution and inheritance**   Test 4 (end of year)

2. **a)** Polar bears live in the Arctic, where it is very cold. The main food of polar bears is seals.

Polar bears catch seals by lying in wait on the ice and snatching them when they come to the surface of the water at a breathing hole. Sometimes polar bears catch seals that are resting on the ice.

fur

body

claws

How are the fur, body and claws of a polar bear adapted to it living in the Arctic?
Write your answers in the boxes.

KU

3 marks

b) Scientists have noticed that the ice in the Arctic is reducing in size. Tick **two** things that could affect how a polar bear survives in its environment.

☐ There would be more icebergs.

☐ It would be easier for the seals to see the polar bear.

☐ The polar bear would not be able to get to the ice to catch the seals.

☐ The sea level would be higher.

KU

2 marks

A

1 mark

c) Over time, what could happen to the polar bear's coat if the climate gets warmer?

/10

Total for this test

© Rising Stars UK Ltd 2014.   You may photocopy this page.

35

Year 6
Light Test 1 (diagnostic)

Name: _____ Class: _____ Date: _____

1. a)

Explain why the child has a shadow.

_____

A
1 mark

b) Circle the object or objects that make a dark shadow.

    stone   tracing paper   glass

KU
1 mark

c) Circle the word that describes a material that lets some light through.

    opaque   transparent   translucent

KU
1 mark

Total for this page

36   © Rising Stars UK Ltd 2014. You may photocopy this page.

2. a) Some children investigate the size of shadows.

Ali   Ben   Carys   wall

Who makes the tallest shadow on the wall?

....

A/WS
1 mark

b) Explain why.

....

A/WS
1 mark

3. Complete the following sentence.

We see an object because .... from the object

....

KU
2 marks

4. Add **two** arrows to this drawing to show how the lamp lets the girl see the glass containing the drink.

lamp

A/WS
2 marks

Total for this page

Year 6 **Light** Test 1 (diagnostic)

5.

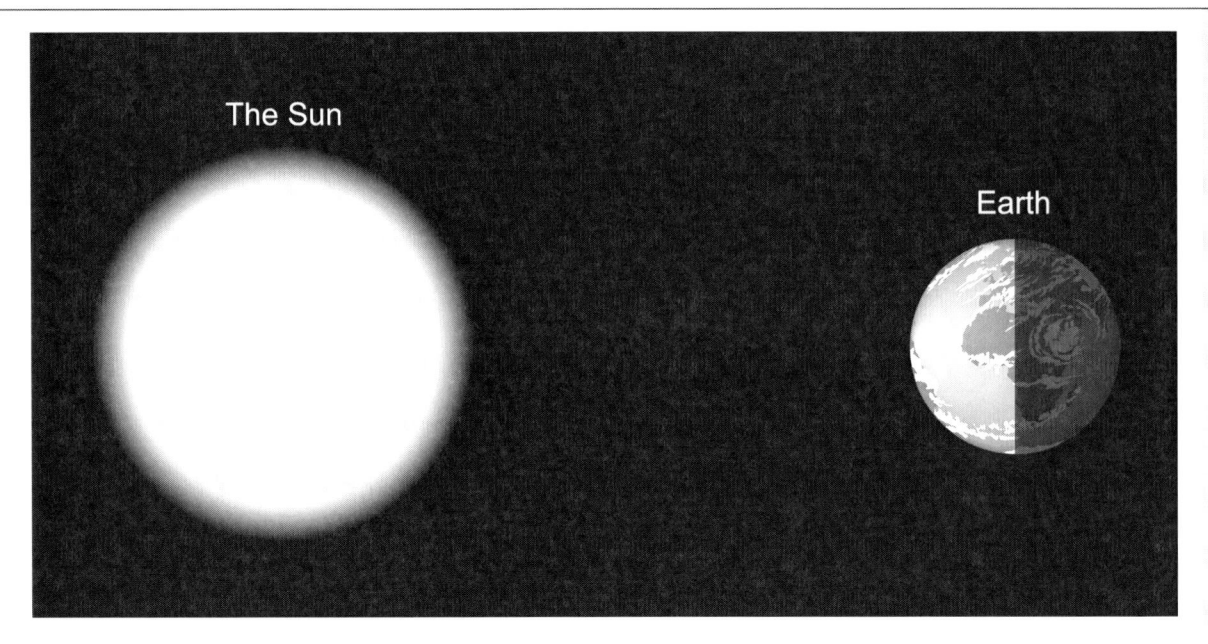

The Sun

Earth

Explain how the light travelling from the Sun in straight lines means that half of the Earth is always in darkness.

KU

1 mark

Year 6
Light Test 2 (mid-topic)

Name: _____ Class: _____ Date: _____

1. **a)** Sam sets up an investigation.

Tick the question Sam is trying to answer.

☐ Can card stop light?

☐ How are shadows formed?

☐ Does light travel in straight lines?

b) What would happen if the holes in the card were smaller?

_____

c) What would happen if the hole in the furthest card from the torch was higher than the other holes?

_____

d) Sam added two more identical pieces to the line of cards. Would the light still go through?

yes ☐   no ☐

© Rising Stars UK Ltd 2014. You may photocopy this page.

Year 6 Light Test 2 (mid-topic)

2. a) Tick the drawing with the correct shadow.

A   B   C

1 mark

b) Why is a shadow formed?

_____

1 mark

c) Circle the type of material that makes the darkest shadow.

    opaque   **transparent**   **translucent**

1 mark

d) Why don't glass window panes make shadows?

_____

1 mark

3. How is a shadow different from a reflection?

_____

_____

_____

2 marks

/10

Total for this test

40

Year 6
Light Test 3 (end of topic)

Name: _____ Class: _____ Date: _____

1. a)

How does the light travel so the cat sees the candle flame?

_____

KU
☐
1 mark

b) Light from the Sun lets the man see the car.

Draw **two** arrows to show how the man sees the car.

KU
☐
2 marks

2. a) Describe how the light travels between the torch and the mirror and how it is reflected.

mirror   torch

_____

KU
☐
1 mark

b) A reflection is when light _____ a shiny surface.

KU
☐
1 mark

☐
Total for this page

© Rising Stars UK Ltd 2014. You may photocopy this page.

41

Year 6 **Light** Test 3 (end of topic)

3.

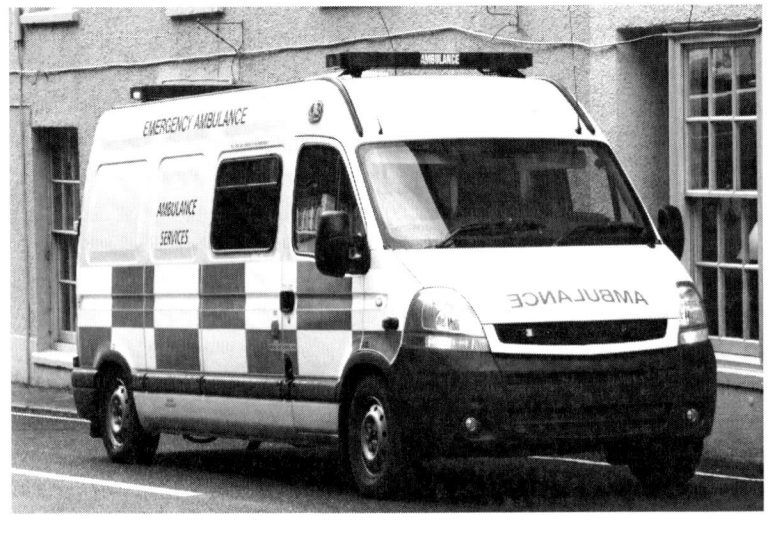

Why do ambulances have writing like this on the front of them?

A

1 mark

4. a) Tom wants to investigate how the distance of the object from the light affects the size of the shadow.

How will he do his investigation?

torch   object

A/WS

1 mark

b) What **two** variables will he measure?

A/WS

2 marks

c) Tom decides to use a line graph to display his results.

Why is a line graph a better choice than a bar chart?

A/WS

1 mark

/10

Total for this test

42   © Rising Stars UK Ltd 2014.   You may photocopy this page.

Year 6
Light Test 4 (end of year)

Name: _____ Class: _____ Date: _____

1. The light lets the boy see the door in the mirror.

   Draw **three** arrows to show how the boy sees the door in the mirror.

   KU

   2 marks

2. a) Class 6 are looking at shadow puppets.

   Tick the picture that shows where the puppet, the light, the screen and the audience need to be.

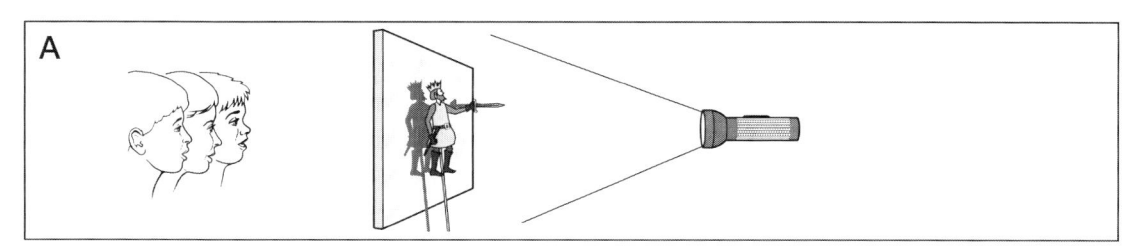

   A

   B

   C

   KU

   1 mark

   Total for this page

© Rising Stars UK Ltd 2014. You may photocopy this page.

43

Year 6 Light Test 4 (end of year)

b) How is the shadow formed?

....

KU

1 mark

c) Ceris thinks the puppeteer makes the shadows bigger by moving the puppet nearer the screen. Dan thinks they are made bigger by moving the puppet away from the screen.

Circle who is right.

      Ceris   **Dan**

KU

1 mark

d) Explain why the size of the shadow changes.

....

....

A

1 mark

e) Class 6 do an investigation to find out who is right.

Tick the equipment they used to do their investigation.

☐ projector   ☐ screen

☐ stopwatch   ☐ puppet

☐ trundle wheel   ☐ tape measure

A/WS

1 mark

Total for this page

f) Here is a graph of their results.

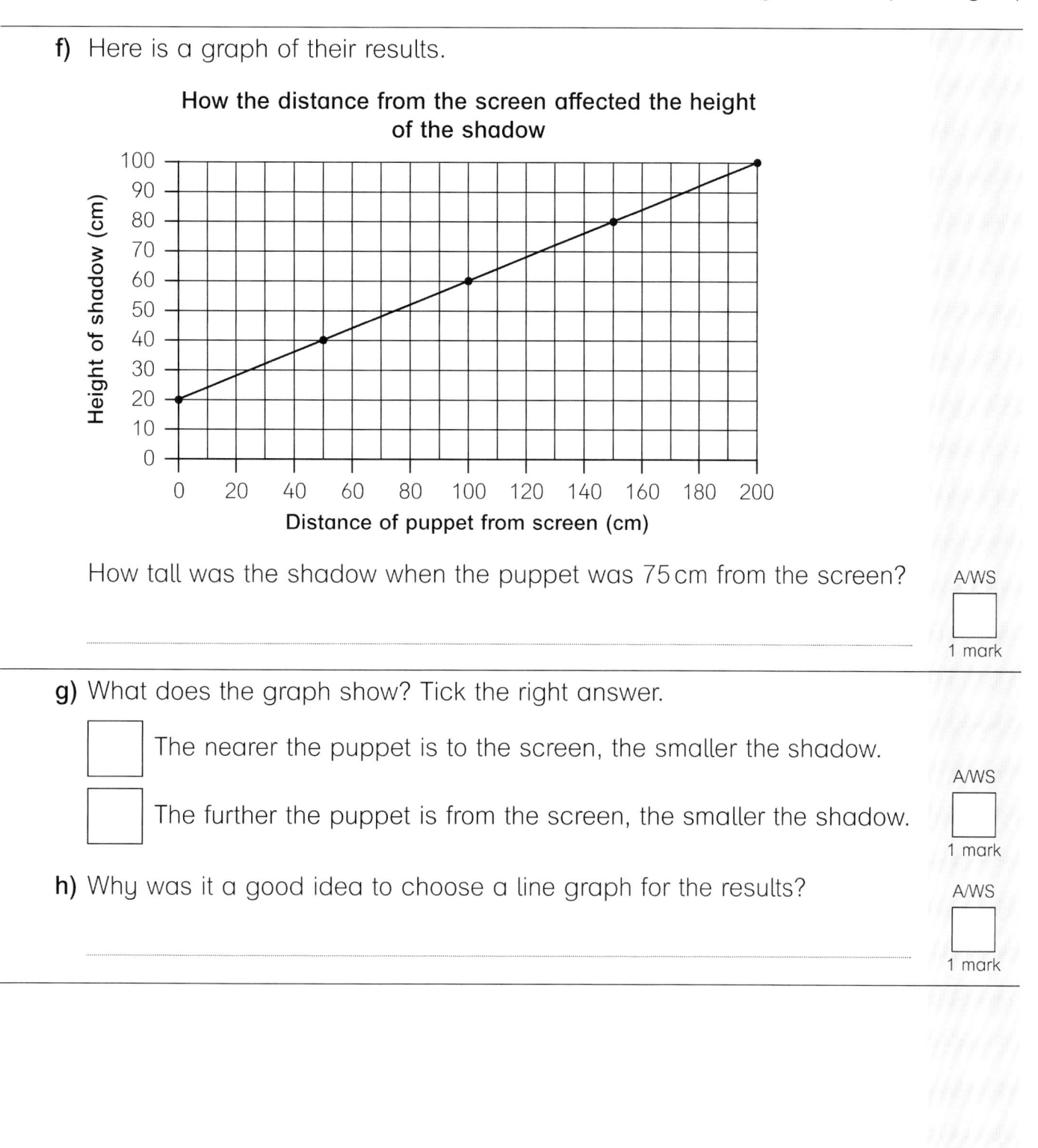

How the distance from the screen affected the height of the shadow

[Line graph: x-axis "Distance of puppet from screen (cm)" 0–200; y-axis "Height of shadow (cm)" 0–100. Points at (0,20), (50,40), (100,60), (150,80), (200,100).]

How tall was the shadow when the puppet was 75 cm from the screen?

....

1 mark

g) What does the graph show? Tick the right answer.

☐ The nearer the puppet is to the screen, the smaller the shadow.

☐ The further the puppet is from the screen, the smaller the shadow.

1 mark

h) Why was it a good idea to choose a line graph for the results?

....

1 mark

/10
Total for this test

Year 6
Electricity Test 1 (diagnostic)

Name: _____ Class: _____ Date: _____

1. Sara is investigating how circuits work.

   a) What happened when she added another bulb to the circuit?

   _____

   A/WS
   ☐
   1 mark

   b) What happened when she added another cell to the circuit with one bulb?

   _____

   A/WS
   ☐
   1 mark

2. a) Draw the symbol for a bulb.

   KU
   ☐
   1 mark

   b) Draw the symbol for a cell.

   KU
   ☐
   1 mark

   ☐
   Total for this page

46 © Rising Stars UK Ltd 2014. You may photocopy this page.

Year 6 **Electricity** Test 1 (diagnostic)

3. Draw a circle around each mistake on this diagram.

KU

2 marks

4. Tick the circuit that will light a bulb.

A   B   C

A

1 mark

5. What is the job of a switch?

KU

....

1 mark

6. Class 6 found out which materials they can use to make a switch for their circuits.

Complete the table by adding a ✓ for materials that Class 6 can use or an ✗ for materials that they can not use.

Material	Good for a switch?
paper	✗
wire	
plastic straw	
tin foil	
lolly stick	

A/WS

2 marks

/10

Total for this test

Year 6
Electricity Test 2 (mid-topic)

Name: _____ Class: _____ Date: _____

1. Class 6 are making circuits. They start by making a simple circuit using one cell, two wires, a bulb and a bulb holder. Leo and Maddy cannot get their bulb to light.

   Suggest **two** reasons why the bulb will not light.

   _____

   _____

   KU ☐ 2 marks

2. Finish the table.

Name	Symbol
wire	——
	─┤├─
bulb	
motor	
	⊥

   KU ☐ 2 marks

3. a) Tom and Jamie used two cells to light two bulbs.

   Tick the circuit diagram that correctly shows the circuit they made.

   A ☐   B ☐   C ☐   D ☐

   A ☐ 1 mark

   ☐ Total for this page

48

Year 6 **Electricity** Test 2 (mid-topic)

b) Tom says that two cells will light six bulbs.

Jamie thinks that two cells will not light this many bulbs.

How should they find out?

_____

_____

A/WS

☐ 1 mark

c) This circuit diagram shows how many bulbs the cells will light.

Was Tom right?

yes ☐   no ☐

A/WS

☐ 1 mark

d) What did they notice about the brightness of the bulbs?

_____

A

☐ 1 mark

e) Complete Jamie's prediction.

If you add another cell _____

A/WS

☐ 1 mark

f) Name **one** piece of equipment that can be used to measure the brightness of a bulb.

_____

KU/WS

☐ 1 mark

/10

Total for this test

Year 6
Electricity Test 3 (end of topic)

Name: _____ Class: _____ Date: _____

1. a) How does a switch work?

   _____

   _____

   KU / 1 mark

   b) Draw the symbols for an open switch and a closed switch.

   | open switch | closed switch |

   KU / 2 marks

   c) If you made a circuit with one cell and two bulbs, would the switch work if you put it between the two bulbs?

   yes ☐   no ☐

   A / 1 mark

2. a) Min constructs a circuit to make her toy roundabout spin.
   Use the correct symbols to draw the circuit she used.

   toy

   A/WS / 2 marks

   Total for this page ☐

50 © Rising Stars UK Ltd 2014. You may photocopy this page.

b) Complete Min's prediction.

To make the roundabout go faster, I could _____

c) What could Min do to see if her prediction is correct?

☐ Add another cell and count how many times the roundabout spins in half a minute.

☐ Count how many times the roundabout spins in half a minute, then add another cell and count it again.

☐ Count how many times the roundabout spins in half a minute, then add another cell.

d) How could Min make the roundabout spin the other way?

_____

3. Give **one** reason why electrical wires have plastic covers.

_____

Year 6
Electricity Test 4 (end of year)

Name: _____ Class: _____ Date: _____

1. Which group of materials are good electrical conductors?
   ....

   KU — 1 mark

2. a) Class 6 are testing how different voltages affect the brightness of a bulb. They use 1.5 V cells.

   Write down **two** things that they can do to help make their test fair.

   ....

   ....

   A/WS — 2 marks

   b) They put their results on a graph.

   How different voltages affect the brightness of a bulb

   (Graph: y-axis "Brightness of bulb"; x-axis "Voltage (V)" with markings 0, 1.5, 3, 4.5, 6, 7.5, 9. Crosses plotted at 1.5 V (low), 4.5 V (medium), 6 V (higher), 7.5 V (zero).)

   Mark on the graph where you think the crosses for 3 V and 9 V would be.

   A/WS — 2 marks

   c) Explain why the reading is zero for 7.5 V.

   ....

   ....

   KU — 1 mark

Total for this page

52 © Rising Stars UK Ltd 2014. You may photocopy this page.

Year 6   **Electricity**   Test 4 (end of year)

3. Sometimes fuses are put into circuits to protect the components.
Explain how a fuse works.

....

....

KU

1 mark

4. Tick the circuits that will work.

A   B   C   D

☐   ☐   ☐   ☐

KU

2 marks

5. Explain why electrical wires are usually made of copper.

....

A

1 mark

/10

Total for this test

Answers and mark schemes

Year 6 Living things and their habitats

Test 1 (diagnostic)		Area	Mark	Extra information
1.	Legs and no legs Six legs or more, and fewer than six legs	A/WS	1	Accept any other two reasonable groupings chosen because of physical characteristics
2.	Mammals: pig, mouse Reptiles: lizard, tortoise, snake	KU	2	2 marks for all correct 1 mark for three or four correct
3a.	*[Key diagram: Are the flowers single? Yes → Do the petals stand upright? No/Yes; No →]*	A/WS	2	2 marks for both correct 1 mark for one correct
3b.	YES/NO all correct on key	A/WS	1	
3c.	To help (make it easier) to identify a plant or animal	KU	1	
4.	Any **two** from: Used to make yoghurt/bread/cheese/alcohol. Used in medicines. Important in compost.	KU	2	
5.	Any **one** from: It has grown. Got bigger/reproduced. It has given off gas/carbon dioxide.	A/WS	1	

Test 2 (mid-topic)		Area	Mark	Extra information
1.	Vertebrates	KU	1	
2a.	mammal – dog bird – swan amphibian – frog reptile – snake fish – cod	A/WS	2	2 marks for all correct 1 mark for three or four correct
2b.	Mammal	A/WS	1	
2c.	Any **one** from: Kangaroos have hair. Kangaroos give birth to live young. Kangaroo mothers feed their babies on breast milk.	A/WS	1	
2d.	They are cold blooded. They have scaly skin.	KU	2	
3.	To help them to identify living things. So that they can see the relationships between different species.	KU	2	
4.	Any **one** from: Cause illness/disease. Rot food/cause decay.	A	1	

© Rising Stars UK Ltd 2014. You may photocopy this page.

Year 6 **Answers and mark schemes**

Living things and their habitats (continued)

Test 3 (end of topic)	Area	Mark	Extra information
1a. Invertebrates	KU	1	
1b. Any **one** from: Most vertebrates would have moved away when they heard the children. There may not be any vertebrates living there. The school garden is not a suitable habitat for a lot of vertebrates.	A	1	
1c. Correct questions entered into key: i) Does it have legs? ii) Does it have wings?/Does it have six legs?	KU	1 1	
1d. Does it have a shell?	A/WS	1	
1e. YES/NO correctly circled on the key	A/WS	2	2 marks for all correct 1 mark for four correct
1f. Any different invertebrate named and put into the correct group on the key, e.g. fly with ladybird; woodlouse with spider; worm with slug.	A/WS	1	
2. Any **two** from: Used to make yoghurt/bread/cheese/alcohol. Used in medicines. Important in compost.	KU	2	

Test 4 (end of year)	Area	Mark	Extra information
1. Any **two** from: It can photosynthesise or make its own food. It has leaves. It has roots	KU	2	Accept it makes oxygen or removes carbon dioxide from air
2a. A fungus is neither a plant nor an animal.	KU	1	
2b. seaweed	KU	1	
2c. Any **one** from: Fungi do not photosynthesise/make their own food. Fungi do not have green leaves. Fungi do not make oxygen.	KU	1	
3. Any **one** from: It does not lay its eggs in water. The young do not live in water when they hatch. It does not breed in water.	A	1	
4a. Any **one** from: Same type of strawberries. Same size strawberries. Same age strawberries. Strawberries washed/wrapped/stored in the same way.	A/WS	1	
4b. With no mould 2°C; strawberry with a little mould 8°C; strawberry with a lot of mould 15°C	A/WS	2	2 marks for all correct 1 mark for one correct
4c. The colder the temperature, the less mould grows or The warmer the temperature the more mould grows.	A/WS	1	Accept: If it is cold not much mould grows or if it is warm more mould grows.

© Rising Stars UK Ltd 2014. You may photocopy this page.

Year 6   Answers and mark schemes

Animals, including humans

Test 1 (diagnostic)	Area	Mark	Extra information
1a. (diagram of human body with X marked on left chest)	KU	1	
1b. Pump blood (around the body)	KU	1	
1c. You are using more energy so you need more oxygen; your muscles need more oxygen or blood	KU	1	Accept any answer that shows the link between more energy being used and the need for more oxygen
2a. The third and fourth groups must be included and the second excluded.	KU	1	The first and fifth groups are optional and are affected by preferences such as vegetarianism or veganism
2b. To be healthy; so your body works properly	A	1	Accept any valid reason
3a. Any **one** from: To keep healthy or fit. To make your muscles strong. It is good for your heart or lungs.	A	1	
3b. no	KU	1	
4a. Ben's	A/WS	1	
4b. yes	A/WS	1	
4c. Any **one** from: They might have made a mistake taking their pulses. It can be difficult to find a pulse so some people may have had a longer rest. Some may have done their star jumps quicker than others.	A/WS	1	

Year 6 Answers and mark schemes

Animals, including humans (continued)

Test 2 (mid-topic)	Area	Mark	Extra information
1a. oxygen	KU	1	
1b. To pump blood (around the body)	KU	1	
1c. The pulse shows: the heartbeat rate; how fast the heart is beating; how (fast) the heart is pumping blood (around the body); how fast the heart is beating	KU	1	Accept any reasonable definition
2. oesophagus	KU	1	
3a. 1:10	A/WS	1	
3b. Any **one** from: His breathing is faster or he is out of breath. He sweats. He can feel his heart beating in his chest.	A	1	
3c. It slowed down; it went back to normal; it returned to its original speed	A/WS	1	Accept any valid description
3d. He was not using so much energy; he had stopped exercising	A/WS	1	Accept any valid explanation
3e. To check his results are reliable	A/WS	1	
4. When they are prescribed by a doctor or given by a parent/carer	KU	1	Do not accept when you are ill

Test 3 (end of topic)	Area	Mark	Extra information
1a. Carbohydrates: pasta, rice, bread Protein: salmon, eggs, chicken	KU	2	2 marks for all correct 1 mark for four or five correct
1b. Any **one** from: Protein helps you grow. Protein helps your body fight infections. Protein helps your blood carry oxygen.	KU	1	
2. They did not get enough vitamins (or minerals).	A	1	Accept that they were not eating a balanced diet
3a. Accept either: How much faster do we breathe when we have run 50 m? Whose breathing rate goes up most/least after exercise?	A/WS	1	Accept any answer that refers to increased breathing rate after exercise
3b. Bess	A/WS	1	
3c. They needed more oxygen (because their bodies were using more energy); their lungs needed to pump more oxygen into their blood	A/WS	1	Accept any answer that refers to the need for more oxygen; do not accept they used more energy
3d. It is difficult to count breathing rate. It is possible to make yourself breathe more slowly.	A/WS	1	1 mark for both correct reasons ticked
4. Any **two** from: cancer; heart disease; lung disease; breathlessness or unable to run as fast/far; smelly breath	KU	2	Do not accept die

© Rising Stars UK Ltd 2014. You may photocopy this page.

Animals, including humans (continued)

Test 4 (end of year)	Area	Mark	Extra information
1. 2. stomach 3. small intestine 4. blood 5. muscles	KU	2	2 marks for all correct 1 mark for two correct
2. Any one from: get fat or put on weight; tooth decay; get spots	KU	1	Do not accept a non-specific answer, e.g. get ill
3. Any **one** from: It loses carbon dioxide. It absorbs oxygen. It exchanges gases. It goes through capillaries.	KU	1	Accept any answer that refers to increased breathing rate after exercise
4a. gone down	A/WS	1	
4b. 1990 and 1995	A/WS	1	
4c. The number has fallen/is falling.	A/WS	1	
4d. Collect/compare information about how many people in the UK smoke now, and compare it with data from previous years.	A/WS	1	
5. Any **one** from: good for heart; strengthens muscles; helps balance; makes you fit; makes you feel good; helps to stop you getting fat	KU	1	
6. damaged liver loss of control	A	1	1 mark for both correct effects ticked

Year 6 Answers and mark schemes

Evolution and inheritance

Test 1 (diagnostic)	Area	Mark	Extra information
1a. The remains or impressions left by a plant or animal that has turned to stone	KU	1	
1b. millions	KU	1	
2. adaptation	KU	1	
3. feet – webbed/big for swimming (fast) in water beak – long/strong/hooked to catch or hold on to fish	A	2	
4a. They have got taller; the height has gone up	A/WS	1	Accept any valid interpretation
4b. 10 cm	A/WS	1	
4c. They had a better diet. There was less illness.	A/WS	2	
5. Any indication that the cat's features are passed on from its parents	KU	1	

Test 2 (mid-topic)	Area	Mark	Extra information
1a. Fossils of it have been found	KU	1	
1b. By the age of the rocks where the fossils were found	A	1	
2. Any **one** from: Loss of habitat. Hunted by other animals. Lack of food. Catastrophic event, e.g. volcano, earthquake.	KU	1	
3a. The remains or impressions left by plants or animals that have turned to stone	KU	1	
3b. 500 million	KU	1	
4a. palaeontologist	KU	1	
4b. Found more bones Compared the bones she found to the skeleton of a crocodile	A/WS	2	
4c. Any physical similarity, e.g. position of limbs; length of spine; length of skull	A/WS	1	
4d. Any physical difference, e.g. shape of head; joints in the legs; amount of ribs	A/WS	1	

© Rising Stars UK Ltd 2014. You may photocopy this page.

Year 6 Answers and mark schemes

Evolution and inheritance (continued)

Test 3 (end of topic)	Area	Mark	Extra information
1a. Any plausible answer, e.g. hair colour, hair length, height, temperament.	A	1	Any one for 1 mark
1b. Any inherited features, e.g. hair colour, straight/curly hair.	A/WS	1	Any one for 1 mark
1c. Any feature caused by surroundings, e.g. if the puppies have any bumps or scratches, teeth marks, hair trimmed.	A/WS	1	Any one for 1 mark
2a. Ben	KU	1	
2b. Eye colour is inherited/genetic	KU	1	Accept an answer that indicates an understanding that eye colour has been passed on, e.g. I have the same colour eyes as my mum/dad/gran/grandad
3a. Plants and animals develop characteristic/features over time that help them survive in their habitats.	KU	1	Do not accept an answer that does not refer to development over time
3b. It has widespread roots. It can store water.	A/WS	2	
4. Any **two** from: They have got taller. Their arms are shorter. They are more upright. They walk on two legs. They are less hairy.	KU	2	

Test 4 (end of year)	Area	Mark	Extra information
1a. sparrow – seeds kestrel – mice heron – fish warbler – insects	A/WS	2	2 marks for all correct 1 mark for two correct
1b. They also found that birds have beaks that are suited to what they eat.	A/WS	1	
1c. A sharp/hooked one to catch/rip its prey	A/WS	1	
2a. fur – white for camouflage or thick to keep it warm body – fat/blubber to keep it warm claws – sharp to help it hold its prey or to grip as it walk on snow and ice	KU	3	
2b. It would be easier for the seals to see the polar bear. The polar bear would not be able to get to the ice to catch the seals.	KU	2	
2c. Go darker Get thinner	A	1	1 mark for one correct answer

Year 6 Answers and mark schemes

Light

Test 1 (diagnostic)	Area	Mark	Extra information
1a. The child is blocking (stopping) the light from the Sun.	A	1	Blocks or stops must be in answer
1b. Stone	KU	1	
1c. Translucent	KU	1	
2a. Ali	A/WS	1	
2b. Ali is nearest the torch and blocks out (stops) more light.	A/WS	1	
3. light enters (reaches) our eyes	KU	2	
4. One arrow drawn from lamp to drink One arrow drawn from drink to girl's eye	A/WS	2	Each arrow must be pointing in the right direction Arrows must be straight and touch the glass/drink
5. The light cannot (bend around to) reach the other side of the Earth.	KU	1	

Test 2 (mid-topic)	Area	Mark	Extra information
1a. Does light travel in straight lines?	A/WS	1	
1b. The light would still come through the holes and/or less light would come through.	A/WS	1	
1c. The light would only go through the first two holes or the third card would stop the light travelling any further.	A/WS	1	
1d. yes	A/WS	1	
2a. B	KU	1	
2b. The object blocks or stops the light or light travels in straight lines and cannot get behind the object.	KU	1	
2c. opaque	KU	1	
2d. The light goes through the glass or the glass is transparent.	A	1	
3. A shadow is formed when an object blocks the light. A reflection is formed when the light bounces off an object.	KU	2	

© Rising Stars UK Ltd 2014. You may photocopy this page.

Year 6 **Answers and mark schemes**

Light (continued)

Test 3 (end of topic)	Area	Mark	Extra information
1a. From the flame to the cat's eyes	KU	1	Accept light travels in a straight line
1b. One arrow drawn from Sun to car One arrow drawn from car to man's eye	KU	2	Each arrow must be pointing in the right direction
2a. It goes from the torch to the mirror and bounces off.	KU	1	Both directions given for 1 mark
2b. Any **one** from: bounces off; is blocked by; is turned by	KU	1	
3. So it can be read in the mirror of the car driving in front or so it is the right way around when it is seen in a mirror.	A	1	
4a. Move the torch away from the object (or move the object away from the torch) and see/measure how big the shadow is	A/WS	1	
4b. Size of the shadow Distance of object from torch	A/WS	2	
4c. He will be able to work out shadow sizes for distances he did not measure more easily	A/WS	1	

Test 4 (end of year)	Area	Mark	Extra information
1. Arrow from light to door Arrow from door to mirror Arrow from mirror to boy	KU	2	2 marks for all arrows correctly drawn 1 mark for two arrows correctly drawn
2a. A	KU	1	
2b. The puppet blocks or stops the light or light travels in straight lines and cannot get behind the puppet.	KU	1	
2c. Dan	KU	1	
2d. When the puppet is further from the screen (nearer the light) it is blocking more light so the shadow is bigger or when the puppet is nearer the screen (further from the light) it is blocking less light so shadow is smaller.	A	1	
2e. projector, screen, puppet, tape measure	A/WS	1	1 mark for all four ticked
2f. 50 cm	A/WS	1	Units needed for 1 mark
2g. The nearer the puppet is to the screen, the smaller the shadow.	A/WS	1	
2h. It shows a pattern in the results or they can work out shadow sizes for distances they did not measure.	A/WS	1	

Year 6 Answers and mark schemes

Electricity

Test 1 (diagnostic)	Area	Mark	Extra information
1a. They were dimmer than when there was only one bulb.	A/WS	1	
1b. The bulb was brighter or the bulb burned out.	A/WS	1	
2a. ⊗	KU	1	
2b. ⊣⊢	KU	1	
3. No wire between two bulbs Wire not joined to cell	KU	2	
4. B	A	1	
5. It completes or makes a circuit (lets the electricity flow) or when open, it breaks a circuit (stops the electricity flowing)	KU	1	
6. Material / Good for a switch? paper ✗ wire ✓ plastic straw ✗ tin foil ✓ lolly stick ✗	A/WS	2	2 marks for all correct 1 mark for two or three correct

Test 2 (mid-topic)	Area	Mark	Extra information
1. Any **two** from: The bulb is broken. The cell (battery) is flat/dead. The circuit is not wired correctly.	KU	2	
2. Name / Symbol wire — — cell or battery ⊣⊢ bulb ⊗ motor Ⓜ buzzer ⌓	KU	2	2 marks for all correct 1 mark for two or three correct
3a. B	A	1	
3b. Keep adding one bulb to the circuit until the bulbs do not light	A/WS	1	
3c. no	A/WS	1	
3d. They got dimmer as they added more bulbs or they were brighter when there were fewer bulbs.	A	1	
3e. The bulbs will be brighter or you will be able to light more bulbs.	A/WS	1	
3f. Any **one** from: light sensor; light meter	KU/WS	1	

© Rising Stars UK Ltd 2014. You may photocopy this page.

Year 6 Answers and mark schemes

Electricity (continued)

Test 3 (end of topic)	Area	Mark	Extra information
1a. When a switch is closed/on, the circuit is complete (or the electricity flows or the bulb lights) or when a switch is open/off, the circuit is broken (or the electricity cannot flow or the bulb is not lit).	KU	1	
1b. —o͡ o— open switch —o—o— closed switch	KU	2	Allow drawings with dots or nothing instead of circles
1c. yes	A	1	
2a. [circuit diagram with cell and motor (M)] Both symbols correctly drawn Straight lines drawn for wires touching the symbols for cell and motor at each side	A/WS	2	
2b. add more cells/batteries	A/WS	1	
2c. Count how many times the roundabout spins in half a minute, then add another cell and count it again.	A/WS	1	
2d. Reverse the wires on the motor or reverse the wires on the cell.	KU	1	
3. Any **one** from: Plastic is an insulator/not a conductor (of electricity). It makes it safe to touch. It stops short circuits.	KU	1	

Test 4 (end of year)	Area	Mark	Extra information
1. Metals	KU	1	
2a. Any two from: Use the same bulb for each test. Use the same type of wires for each test. Use the same length of wire for each test. Use the same type of cells for each test.	A/WS	2	
2b. X for 3V is at a height approximately halfway between the height of X for 1.5V and 4.5V. X for 9V is on x-axis (i.e. at zero).	A/WS	2	
2c. The bulb has burned out/broken	KU	1	
3. A fuse contains a thin strip of wire that melts and breaks the circuit if the current gets too big.	KU	1	
4. C D	KU	2	
5. Copper is a conductor (of electricity) or it allows the electricity to pass through.	A	1	